EARLY PRAISE FOR "HOW TO BE

'A must-read guide for all aspiring COOs. Packed with practical insights and based on real life experiences, it gives a clear and powerful road map for this transformational organizational role.'
Justin Forsyth, Deputy Executive Director, UNICEF

'It is rare for a single book to command such breadth of expertise, practical insight and advice that is so easy to put into action. This is a consequence of the superb clarity of Jennifer's writing, and the fact that she has earned her expertise – and the scars that come with it – from working on the business end of the stick for over twenty years.'
Mark Waddington, CEO, Hope and Homes for Children

'Crisply written, clear and to the point.'
Ben Brabyn, CEO, Level 39

'An impressive read. De-codes the very tricky role of COO and inspires you on how to be a great one.'
Niamh O'Keeffe, Author of "Your First 100 days" and "Your Next Role"

'The defining text on the role of the COO and its component parts. This is an informative and useful read for existing COOs. It is a must read for new COOs, aspiring COOs and most importantly CEOs and Heads of HR in hiring COOs for their organisations.'
Paul Ford, CEO, Anchura Partners

'The role of COO is a balancing act, and requires multiple hard and soft skills. This nifty handbook provides a shortcut to understand the critical skills required, and is filled with nuggets of practical and accessible advice.'
Sinead Mahon, Banking COO

'This book takes one of the most frameless and unstructured roles in business today, and using personal experiences seeks to help others to demystify the role and deliver insight on how to be effective and successful. Insightful and extensive, a book I would have loved to have access to when I was starting out in my career.'
Pam Murphy, COO, Infor

HOW TO BE A CHIEF OPERATING OFFICER

16 disciplines for success

JENNIFER GEARY

For more information about the author and further materials, visit www.coo-author.com

ISBN: 978-1-9997683-0-0 (e-book)

ISBN: 978-1-9997683-1-7 (print)

DEDICATION

To Conor. Thank you for everything. I love you.

To Mum (RIP) and Dad. I hope this makes you proud.

To Jack and Anna. Believe in yourselves, my darlings, and you can do anything.

Contents

Author's acknowledgements

I wanted this book to be as strong as it could possibly be. A dream team of technical experts has kindly given its time to interrogate my content, flesh out my theories and challenge my thinking. Their input has made this book stronger and more robust.

I would therefore like to thank the named technical reviewers below, and also those who chose to contribute anonymously. Many thanks also to my editor, Spencer Borup, Catherine Kiely, David Imran of Accenture, Sarah Walsh, and my coach, Paula Boyle. Thank you to Lucy Buck and Jo Ralling, who helped me see the true potential of this book, and give it its name. Huge thanks to Vikki, who makes our life run like clockwork and who gave me the space to get this book out of my head.

Finally, thanks to RE Vance, Chandler Bolt, Sean Sumner and my fellow students at the Self-Publishing school for opening up the possibility of self-publishing to me.

ABOUT THE AUTHOR

Jennifer Geary is a COO with over 20 years' experience in finance, technology, risk and legal, across diverse industries from financial services to not-for-profit. After gaining a Bachelor of Commerce and Masters of Accounting at University College Dublin, she trained as a Chartered Accountant with a global accounting firm in Dublin, where she won an award for the design of her Technology Risk assessment diagnostic. She subsequently moved to New York to deliver risk-based consultancy for financial services clients, including the rollout of a trading surveillance system for a major Wall Street investment bank.

In 2002 she came to London where she spent 13 years in Barclays, initially in Investment Banking where she strengthened the IT controls framework and delivered technology solutions to the Equity Derivatives team, followed by Wealth Management where she assembled and led a global Risk and Governance team, and finally as Chief of Staff to the Group General Counsel where she supported the harmonisation of legal services for the Barclays group. Having long held an interest in corporate social responsibility and sustainability, she seized an opportunity to serve as Chief Operating Officer of Save the Children UK, a £400m NGO, which serves in 68 countries and helps 22 million children every year. She helped the organisation define its new strategy and business plan, oversaw the implementation of key technology platforms, and upgraded its facilities and agile working capabilities.

Jennifer is a Fellow of the Institute of Chartered Accountants in Ireland, PRINCE 2 foundation and practitioner certified, and has attained the CISA and CISSP accreditations. She is a Trustee of the Board of Child's I Foundation. When not working or writing, she can be found falling off a surfboard, finding her zen through yoga, running, swimming, or hanging out with her family. Jennifer lives in London with her husband and two children.

You can connect with Jennifer at www.coo-author.com.

ABOUT THE TECHNICAL REVIEWERS

Jacqui Alexander - Culture, Strategy and Change. Jacqui Alexander is Managing Director of ChangePace Consulting Ltd, a provider of services that create a contagious commitment to change in organisations. She is an award-winning expert with 30 years of business transformation experience and a proven track record of delivering improved business results.

Duncan Perry - Legal, Governance and Compliance. Duncan is a qualified lawyer of 25 years standing with a decade of experience in leading London and New York law firms. He has held senior General Counsel and COO positions at an Investment bank, a hedge fund and at a leading UK Wealth Manager.

Paul Cutler – HR. Paul Cutler has operated at executive level in HR at all scales of business from global enterprises to start-ups, across the private and not-for-profit sectors. His consultancy Mandala.uk.com helps people and organisations to increase performance by seeking purpose and fulfilling potential.

Ardell Bunt - Facilities and Real estate. Ardell has held key roles in contracting, consulting and client organisations for 25 years. He has run his own corporate advisory business and recently returned to lead IFM sales and solutioning for a major EMEA client.

Lauren Iannarone – Corporate Social Responsibility. Lauren has over 20 years of global experience advising public policy and corporate leaders on a wide range of sustainability and corporate affairs strategies. She has held posts in numerous sectors including energy, banking, and consumer products, as well as software and technology.

Jeremy Robinson – Jeremy Robinson has over 30 years of supply chain experience, having worked across many industry sectors such as Financial Services, Consumer Goods, Utilities, Telecoms and Retail in both line management and consulting roles, latterly with Accenture. Jeremy is now the Director of Supply Chain for Save the Children, one of the largest not-for-profit organisations in the sector.

INTRODUCTION

Chief Operating Officers face a near-impossible task. In addition to being the number-two person in the organisation and enjoying a close and successful working relationship with their CEO, they are expected to be knowledgeable across an incredibly broad range of disciplines: technology, human resources, compliance, facilities management, and so on. Once they grasp the basics of each discipline, they have to thoughtfully and judiciously apply their time, effort and political capital in the right quantities to each of these departments, in order to drive the organisation forward.

COO is one of the most difficult, challenging and diverse roles that exist in business. But unlike CEOs, CROs or CFOs, COOs have no established framework or body of knowledge to support them. There are very few resources to help them on their journey. This book seeks to address that gap by equipping COOs with 16 core elements for success—the 3 fundamental pillars of culture, strategy and change, plus expertise in 13 technical areas.

Before securing my first COO role, I worked for over 20 years in the following disciplines: accounting, operational risk, technology programme delivery, chief of staff, a global risk function, and legal. Even with this breadth of experience, when I started as a COO, I was acutely aware that I was being asked to lead teams for the first time in disciplines I had only tangential knowledge of: HR, Communications, Insurance, Facilities Management, and more. I had to work hard, dig deep, and read voraciously. I reached out to contacts for subject matter knowledge, built a trusted community of advisors, and gradually moved up the learning curve. I thought there must be a better way. This is what prompted me to write this book—it's the book I wish I had at the outset.

In writing this book, apart from drawing on my own hard-won knowledge, I have also consulted with functional experts to ensure that what follows is as accurate and as up-to-date as it can be. I have road-tested the breadth of the content with people in different sectors, all of whom said they wish they had this book on day one. In concise, pithy terms, this book will give you enough of what you need to know to establish yourself, build relationships, and get started. You won't qualify for a PhD (you don't need to), but you'll have enough of an understanding of each discipline to set yourself up for success. Whether you're aspiring or an experienced COO, this book will jumpstart your knowledge, equip you with the tools to quickly identify problem areas, help you build those all-important relationships with your heads of departments, and get you well on your way.

You are busy and your time is precious. In these important early days, you have to ration your time effectively. I believe that the few hours' investment in reading this book will pay you back a hundredfold. It will boost your confidence, solidify your standing, and tune your attention to where to place early focus. For each department, as well as outlining the roles and responsibilities of each area, I'll provide you with an insight into some early warning signs for potential problems. I'll highlight the areas where the roles tend to overlap or to interfere with one another. I'll equip you with industry-standard frameworks against which you can benchmark your departments, and I'll give you some of the current hot topics that likely occupy the minds of your department heads.

As a new COO, whether or not you publish a formal 100 day plan, you'll have about that much time to settle in, establish your credibility, build relationships, and decide what areas need your attention. This book will help you hit the ground running. There is no time to lose. I wish you well.

About this book

Every COO has gaps in their knowledge. This book will help you fill those gaps by giving you enough information about a wide range of disciplines, enabling you to have an informed conversation with any subject matter expert in any chosen field. It's written in straightforward English, with terms explained and referenced.

Each chapter is structured along the following lines:

- **What this department does.** A simple outline as to what this department is responsible for.
- **Roles and responsibilities.** A structured list of functions that your head of department is usually responsible for. I have highlighted responsibilities that can sit in alternative areas. I've also highlighted **overlaps** with other departments and key **relationships to watch**—areas where you may need to play the role of referee.
- **Industry frameworks.** I've called out established industry norms and frameworks that you may need to comply with. Even if not mandated, they will provide useful benchmarks against which you can assess the effectiveness of the department.
- **Warning signs.** This section contains a list of common warning signs that may indicate all is not well and highlight departments that need your attention.
- **Good to great.** After establishing that a department is working well, here you'll find tips on how you can elevate

it further, challenging and empowering your leader and team.

- **Current hot topics.** A list of topics that are particularly relevant for this department at the time of writing.
- **Key policies.** A checklist of the policies you can expect in this area and should review during your first 100 days.
- **Ten questions to ask.** A list of ten key questions to ask your department heads in your initial meetings. The answers to these questions will tell you a lot about the department itself and the person leading it.
- **Further reading**. A number of classic texts and up-to-date articles to deepen your understanding.

Your feedback

This book aims to cover a lot in a short read. Inevitably, there will be gaps and areas you as a reader might like to see more of. I would greatly welcome your feedback. Please go to www.coo-author.com and let me know which sections you liked, what you'd like to see more of, and any other comments. In return, as well as taking your feedback on board, I will make a £1 donation to Child's I Foundation for every piece of feedback received.

Section 1: The foundations

The bulk of this book is concerned with the technical disciplines a COO is required to be competent in, in order to be effective. However, before we get into those, there are some foundations we need to cover.

First, a good COO must be self-aware. They must know what the organisation requires from its COO, and how well they fit that mould. They must be cognisant of their own strengths and areas for development, and set up the appropriate support.

Second, everything the COO does must be underpinned by the pillars of Culture, Strategy and Change. These chapters cover how a COO diagnoses these areas and how they tailor their approach according to the situation in the organisation. Once these are established, then the COO can turn their mind to the individual departments under their remit.

1. BEFORE YOU BEGIN

Chief Operating Officer is likely one of the biggest roles you've ever taken on. The CEO, the Board of Directors, the shareholders and staff are all going to need you to be at the top of your game; clear-headed, motivated, and energetic. You owe it to them to optimise your preparation.

Every role has to start with a strong foundation. This chapter will help you establish the following:

- Key character traits of a COO
- The kind of a COO your organisation needs
- The kind of a COO you want to be
- The areas where your knowledge needs bolstering
- What to do if you have a crisis of confidence

Once you land in your role, you'll be expected to hit the ground running. If you fail to prepare, you'll fail to optimise your role. It can be difficult to recover from that position. If you're still carrying baggage from your last job, both physical and emotional, you'll quickly tire and won't be able to approach your new job with the right mind-set. You can recover from a shaky start – many people have done so. However, it's so much easier if you start well. If, by the end of your first 100 days, you have got to know your team, identified strong and weak areas, started to build trusting relationships, and got the team moving forward in the right direction, you have great momentum which will stand to you for the duration of your role.

Preparation for your new role

Taking adequate time to prepare for your new role is critical. During this time, you can do some in-depth reading, thinking, and letting go of your old role. Use this time to set preliminary goals. They'll be refined and tweaked once you start your new job, but having thought of them ahead of time is enormously grounding.

> Over the past ten years, as I've taken on increasingly senior roles, I created a habit of taking a two-day break to prepare myself for the new role. I take myself away somewhere, packing whatever reading I've been given, notebooks, pens, yoga gear, and some tried-and-tested tools to help me get ready. It's a ritual that has served me well. I now look forward to it in advance of any new role.

It's very important to structure your first 100 days. After you set yourself goals, work backward in time and write a goal for each month, week, and even day. Later you can use it to help you focus and hold yourself accountable. It's a powerful habit that will stand you in good stead. 'Your First 100 Days: How to make maximum impact in your new role' by Niamh O'Keeffe is an excellent book that provides exactly this framework.

Counterintuitive as it may seem, it's important that you start your role knowing what a successful ending looks like. You should take the time to develop a sense of your legacy. This is a great conversation to have during your interview. "If I'm successful in this role, what will this organisation look like in three years' time?"

In "Your first 100 days", the author recommends that you "start with the end in mind" and work your plans back from that point. Set your legacy, then translate it back into what you need to get done in your first 100 days, month by month.

Once you have these goals, you need to design a regular habit of reviewing them and holding yourself accountable.

Daily habits

I have a morning routine where I set myself up for the day, personally and professionally, physically and mentally. It has made me strong and focused. It comes from the book 'The Miracle Morning: The Not-So-Obvious Secret Guaranteed to Transform Your Life (Before 8AM)' by Hal Elrod. In his book Elrod covers six activities known as "SAVERS": Silence (or meditation), Affirmations, Visualisation, Exercise, Reading and Scribing (or journaling). Once you set your plan for your new role, you can use this regular preparation time to remind yourself of what you're looking to achieve that week and that day, before you get swamped in back-to-back meetings all day. It will help you keep hold of your own agenda while still making yourself available to others.

Another crucial part of this preparation is deciding how you'll achieve work-life balance. Your role is likely to be highly demanding, particularly at the outset. This doesn't mean you should forego exercise and extra-curricular activity. You're paid to lead, not to be miserable and exhausted. Planning how you'll de-compress, stay fit and healthy and maintain a sense of balance in your life is a necessity. It's also an important signal to your staff about your outlook on work. If you show up looking grey and tired, first to arrive and last to leave, if you repeatedly miss family events, lose your good humour and your perspective, your staff will think that's what you expect of them too, no matter what you say. Lead by example. Decide, right now, that you're going to work hard *and* to have a good life.

A great assistant and, possibly, a Chief of Staff are crucial to your success. Whether you're inheriting support staff in the new role, or bringing them with you, these people will be the difference between you achieving your plans and not. They'll optimise your diary, filtering out the nice-to-have items from the essentials. They'll ensure you have time for reflection. They'll hold you accountable to spending enough time on coaching and inspiring your people, on blue-sky thinking and on strategizing. Bring them into your confidence; discuss with them what visits you need to make in your first three months, who you need to spend time with, and which events and meetings you can shelve. Hire these people early and use them—they'll be indispensable. In his book 'Chief of Staff: The Strategic Partner Who Will Revolutionize Your Organization' Tyler Parris lists the benefits of having a Chief of Staff and how to use them successfully.

Character traits of a COO

As you'll see later in the chapter, there are different kinds of COO, depending on the organisation's needs, the relationship with the CEO and the departments they're responsible for. However, there are some character traits that are essential for all COOs to be effective and to thrive in their roles.

Resilience

The COO role is thankless. When things go well, people take it as a given. When things go wrong, people often view it as your fault, and it will likely be your responsibility to fix the problem. You need a very strong foundation and a groundswell of resilience to stay positive and focused.

COOs have to be adaptable and flexible—the goalposts move all the time. You can't hold on to previous models or misconceptions. You have to be able to let things go with good humour and immediately focus on new goals. As EY say in their article "The DNA of the COO – time to claim the spotlight", 'When the company's Plan A doesn't work out as hoped, the COO needs to be the person who already has a Plan B in mind.'

As a COO you have to be prepared to:

- learn fast
- embrace new areas and new disciplines
- apply your knowledge and wisdom to new contexts
- see common themes
- create a plan
- move quickly, reassuring your people along the way

You need to be the sort of person who can be dropped into an unholy mess, quickly make sense of it, see key issues, discard distractions, clarify the way forward, develop a plan and get people executing on it, fast.

You need to be able to receive bad news (sometimes quite regularly), react to it appropriately, and then convey it courageously to your CEO and Board of Directors, owning the message and the remediation plan. You need to cover for people when they have let you down, even if you're angry and disappointed. You need to manage your negative feelings and turn setbacks into opportunities for learning and improvement.

Finally, at your core, you must be a positive person who believes in the best but expects the worst, who loves the mission of the organisation and the people who work there. Without this your effectiveness will quickly erode.

If you're entering your first COO role, you need to get accustomed to a certain ongoing level of anxiety. Whether you work in a highly sophisticated financial services organisation, or in a fledgling start-up, you'll be faced with things going wrong regularly. From building health and safety issues to regulatory compliance, from people issues to litigation, you're the filter to your CEO. You must protect your CEO so they can advance the mission of the organisation. How you cope will determine your effectiveness in this role. That said, you're a problem solver or you wouldn't be in this role, and there is a great satisfaction in dealing with these potential issues, improving your organization, and striking risks off your worry list.

Execution focus

As an effective COO you must have a ruthless, dogged focus on execution. You must be tenacious and persistent. You must be outcome-focused, directing the conversation towards the logical next step that will move your organization in the direction of the goal you're seeking to accomplish. Often to you, this is invisible and obvious, but to your organisation it's highly valuable. Execution is the translation of vision into action. It's the clutch in the gearbox that drives the engine forward.

Humanity

A dogged focus on delivery doesn't mean you can't be kind or empathetic. In fact, the most impactful people I have worked with balance their focus on execution with warmth and humility. They view their people as people. They know about their lives, their families, and their challenges outside of work. They know what their people want to get out of life, and they want to help them achieve their goals.

For many years in my earlier career, I suppressed that side of myself, and so did the people I worked with. It makes for a grey, flat, joyless existence. I remember returning to the office from a family funeral and nobody, not one person in my team, asking me if I was okay. Financial reward may buy people's compliance but it won't buy their hearts and minds. When people see your humanity shining through, they empathise with you, they buy into the authenticity they're seeing and they understand, even when you're being tough, that you're doing it from a good place.

An ability to hack the system

A COO is in prime position to look across the organisation, filter out the noise, see opportunities and make connections. Effective COOs can see where there are bottlenecks, shortcomings and inefficiencies in an organisation and find ways to remediate them. A good COO is not satisfied with sub-optimal procedures and can "hack" the organisation to achieve better results.

Multi-threading

As a COO you can find yourself reporting to a Board member one minute and dealing with an operational issue the next. You need dexterity of mind to constantly shift perspective and tailor your responses to different situation. You'll also need humility to be able to just get on with things.

I recently heard a talk given by serial entrepreneur Gary Vaynerchuk where he talked about 'clouds and dirt.' He explained that successful leaders switch between thinking strategically and dealing with the minutiae very quickly, thousands of times a day.

Your role will embrace things from the sublime to the ridiculous. Don't be surprised if one minute you're forming a new strategic vision and the next you're being told about an issue with the bathrooms. Just get on with it. Of course, if too much operational work is getting in the way, you need to ask yourself why and address it—one of the things I'll tackle in the "Warning Signs" section of each chapter.

A generalist

No doubt, you will be coming to your role with strong knowledge of some technical areas. Now you need to have a working knowledge of all of them, which is where this book comes in. Later in this chapter, I'll take you through a self-assessment where you can analyse your comfort levels across all the functions you now have to oversee.

Self-awareness

A COO is often the go-to person for all of the organisation's problems. This constant bombardment with issues can be exhausting. It can lead to an always-on, fire-fighting mentality where you're constantly swatting away problems, space-invaders style. This is not conducive to thinking and can impair the very clarity of vision you were hired for.

You need to adopt coping mechanisms that suit your personality type. You need an excellent executive assistant who will understand your needs and will manage your diary accordingly. You need family support and downtime. You need escapes—both quick ones (walking around the park) and periodic ones (such as getting to the coast once a month). You need time for deep thought and strategizing. And you need to have fun. If you become drained, bitter, brittle and reactive, you won't be effective.

If you don't have a personal coach, I suggest now is a good time to find one. A coach will help you develop self-awareness, find out what sets you off, and teach you how to cope with stressful situations.

Some years ago, I found a particularly useful set of concepts in a book called "Complex IT Project Management: 16 Steps to Success" by Peter Schulte. I typed up my favourite phrases to refer to when needed:

"Grace under fire"

"Be the project adult"

"Self-discipline, self-control, tolerance and the knowledge and willingness to be empathetic and gracious towards others are... the marks of a mature person"

"Do not expect much in the way of accolades"

Having these concepts close at hand in challenging moments has proven a sound coping strategy. Can you identify the triggers that set you off? Do you know what can help you in that moment? If you don't, it might be a good opportunity to reflect and prepare.

Reflection

- How are you feeling physically, mentally, emotionally?
- Do you have your support network around you: mentors, coaches, family, friends, sounding boards, childcare professionals?
- Is there any help you'd like to get now, to work through any kinks in your first 100 days on the job?
- How much time can you take to prepare?

- Have you "emptied your suitcases" from your previous role?
- Can you set yourself up to have a core of strength, positivity, empathy, gratitude, warmth and humanity?

What does the organisation need from its COO?

One key point of reflection during your preparation time is to consider what the organisation is going to need from you once you're the COO. This varies enormously from organisation to organisation, and even over time. The COO who was in position during the heady growth days may not be the right person during a time of retrenchment. In fact, it's often helpful to change COOs at key points of inflection in the organisation, to mark a change and draw a line under the previous era.

To help frame your thoughts, it's useful to look at what has been written about the role of the COO. In "Aiming for the top: A guide for aspiring COOs and their organizations", EY (Ernst & Young)[1] note that the scope and the role of the COO position vary widely, depending on four factors:

1. Specific pressures faced by the organisation
2. Key industry trends
3. Relationship with the CEO
4. Organisation structure

---

[1] "Aiming for the top: A guide for aspiring COOs and their organizations." Ernst & Young. September 23, 2013. Accessed May 18, 2017.
http://www.ey.com/Publication/vwLUAssets/Aiming_for_the_top/$FILE/EY-Aiming-for-the-top.pdf.

Nonetheless, EY categorised the common functions of a COO into Development, Enablement and Execution, and plotted six sub-functions against them.

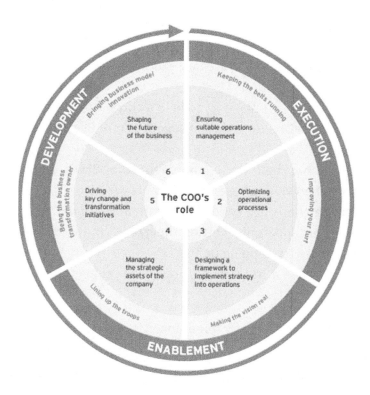

It also identified seven core skills that any prospective COO needs to have:

1. Mastery of change management
2. Engaging in strategic board-level discussions
3. Setting and enforcing robust operational controls
4. Designing and implementing the organisation's operati~~~~~ model
5. Proficiency in identifying and extracting
6. Deep industry and market knowledge

7. Finding a multicultural management approach

The Harvard Business Review article "Second in Command: The Misunderstood Role of the Chief Operating Officer" outlines seven different types of COO:[2]

1. The executor of strategies—turning a vision into reality through execution
2. The change agent—e.g., to lead a corporate turnaround
3. The mentor—to a perhaps younger or less experienced CEO
4. The other half—to complement the CEO's experience, style, knowledge base or penchants
5. The partner—in a co-leadership model with the CEO
6. The heir apparent—cutting their teeth in the number two role prior to stepping up to CEO
7. The MVP—a role given to an executive deemed too valuable to lose

The article also gives a very good analysis of what the COO owes the CEO in their relationship and vice versa. Agreeing to these parameters up front with your CEO will provide you with a solid foundation for the future.

Reflection:

- Where is the organisation on its journey (start-up, growth, cutbacks, crisis)?
- What is the strategy of the organisation?

---

[2] Bennett, Nathan, and Stephen A. Miles. "Second in Command: The Misunderstood Role of the Chief Operating Officer." *Harvard Business Review*, 2006. Accessed May 18, 2017. https://hbr.org/2006/05/second-in-and-the-misunderstood-role-of-the-chief-operating-officer.

- How have your responsibilities been defined?
- What would a "good" year look like in terms of your performance?
- What role will you play vs. your CEO?

What kind of COO do you want to be?

Leaving aside the tangible requirements of the role, it's important to recognise that you have a choice about the kind of person and COO you want to be.

This may be the biggest position of your career. You'll find that your words and actions will wield more potency than ever before, both inside and outside the organisation. People will look to you for cues and emulate your behaviour. People will take your phone calls and prioritise the meetings with you. You'll enjoy more presence, power and influence than ever before, and you'll have more autonomy to shape the future direction of the organisation and sector you work in.

With this privilege comes responsibility. You can choose to be Machiavellian, to win at all costs. You can eradicate competition. You can end careers. You can disregard sustainability. You can squeeze the weaker players in your supply chain into submission. Worse, you can pay lip service to all the good, nice concepts in the world, then turn around and choose the toxic route.

Or you can stand for something. You can be a beacon of integrity and bravery. You can make the hard, right decisions. You can find mutually beneficial solutions. You can enrich the lives of your staff, customers, suppliers and everyone else who interacts with your organisation. You can send people home happy. You can be strong and courageous.

The character traits that you possess will be amplified by this role. Your words and actions will resonate more than ever. Make them good ones.

Reflection

- What will you be known for as a COO?
- What will people say about you after you're gone?

What functional knowledge do you need?

The role of the COO is incredibly varied. You may have some or all of the departments I mention below under your remit. Take a moment to reflect on how comfortable you are feeling with the subject matter in each area. Nobody else has to see it! Be honest with yourself—list where you feel prepared and where you feel less so. It will give you a structured plan to quickly assimilate the knowledge you'll need to get started. Review the areas below and answer on a scale of 1-10 (1=no knowledge, 10=world authority) how well you know the area. Answer N/A if it's not relevant to you.

Area	Score
Culture	
Strategy	
Change	

Department	Score
IT	
Finance	
Risk	
Governance	
Legal	
HR	
Compliance	
Operations	
Supply Chain Management	
Communications / Public Relations	
Facilities Management	
Child safeguarding / Safeguarding of vulnerable people	
Other	

The remainder of this book is structured to support you in rounding up your lower scores and consolidating your stronger ones. You don't need to read the chapters in order—read them as you see fit and score yourself after each chapter to determine which chapter you should read next. I also include a list of recommended reading at the end of each chapter.

Reflection

- Having assessed your knowledge, where do you need to prioritise your learning?

When all else fails

On bad days, you may suffer a crisis of confidence, or even imposter syndrome. I've spoken to enough senior executives to know that everyone goes through this. When you feel this way, remember that (1) you know a lot more than you think you do, and (2) the following five things require no skill or expertise whatsoever, and they count for a lot.

1. **Be polite.** This means—be on time and be prepared. Read the content you've been given in advance and ask only key questions.
2. **Go the extra mile.** Show up with a hard work ethic. People will see it, appreciate it, and emulate it.
3. **Bring energy and show up with passion.** Reflect this in your body language, your energy, and your attitude. Show interest in the topic, read and research it ahead of time.
4. **Be adaptable and open to change**. Take feedback from people whose opinion you value. Get a coach, listen to them with humility, and take things on board.
5. **Be kind and human.** The task at hand will come and go. Human relationships endure. How we act, particularly under pressure, is what people will remember.

On tough days, get up early, exercise, and think about the positive sides of your role. Remember that it's an utter privilege to do your job, then grab a coffee and get back in there.

Further reading

Elrod, H., *"The Miracle Morning: The Not-So-Obvious Secret Guaranteed to Transform Your Life (Before 8am)"*, John Murray Learning, 1st ed., 2016

O'Keeffe, N., "Your First 100 Days: How to make maximum impact in your new leadership role", Financial Times Series, 2011

Parris, T., "Chief of Staff: The Strategic Partner Who Will Revolutionize Your Organization", 2015

Schulte, P., "Complex IT Project Management: 16 Steps to Success", CRC press 2003

"Second in Command: The Misunderstood role of the Chief Operating Officer." *Harvard Business Review*

"The DNA of the COO: Time to claim the spotlight." *Ernst & Young*

"Aiming for the top: A guide for aspiring COOs and their organizations." *Ernst & Young*

2. Culture

Nothing focuses the mind on culture more than trying to lead people who are not motivated by money. When I moved from a hardcore financial services organisation with an annual bonus culture to an NGO (non-governmental organisation), the contrast in how to motivate and engage the staff was stark. In banking (and this applies across the industry) the culture can be very orderly and obedient—the leaders set the direction, the staff look up, nod, get back to their desks and work furiously, in the hope that at the end of the year they'll be rewarded by their line manager. In an NGO, people have often taken a pay cut to come to the organisation. They are highly idealistic and values-driven. Because of that idealism, some can become disillusioned and cynical. Money doesn't work. Expecting obedience doesn't work. Many of the levers that you have in a traditional organisation simply aren't there, or you pull them and nothing happens – indeed, sometimes they can have the opposite of the intended effect.

Ignore culture at your peril. It's the invisible ether in the organisation. It impacts everything. You should ask as many questions and take as many sounding points as you possibly can about the culture of an organisation, both before and after joining it.

As a COO you'll have to tailor your approach depending on the culture. If the culture is weak, you'll have to invest time in strengthening and defining it. If it's positive, your initiatives will take flight faster. If it's negative and resistant to change, it may take much longer to see any of your initiatives embedded. Culture is the glue that holds everything together. It's the hidden mojo behind success or failure. It has been said that 70% of the behaviour exhibited by people in organisations is shaped by the culture—they will act as different people based on the culture around them.

Remuneration strategy and employee benefits lose their motivational power if the culture is bad. Employees typically work 220 days a year. Every day the culture of the organisation hits them in a hundred different ways: the tone of the e-mails they receive, the conversations they overhear, and so on. They get paid 12 times a year and spend that money mainly on necessities. They go on holidays a couple of times a year. They see and feel culture every minute of every working day.

What is culture

A generally accepted definition of culture is "a system of shared **assumptions, values** and **beliefs**, which governs how people behave in organisations." In *Organizational Culture and Leadership,* Edgar H. Schein says that we can think of culture as "what the group has learned in its efforts to survive, grow, deal with its external environment, and organize itself."[3] According to David Needle[4], the following factors combine to shape the culture of an organisation:

---

[3] Schein, Edgar H. *Organizational Culture and Leadership.* 5th ed. Wiley, 2016.
[4] Needle, David. *Business in Context: An Introduction to Business and Its Environment.* 6th ed. Cengage Learning EMEA, 2015.

- History
- Product
- Market
- Technology
- Strategy
- Type of employees
- Management style
- National culture

Note, management style is just one of eight factors! The tone you set as a COO is a key determinant of culture, but by no means the only one. Because culture is shaped by the history and the strategy of the organisation, it can be notoriously slow and difficult to change. It can also be damaged. Like that other valuable attribute, reputation, it's slow to build and easy to fracture. Hold it carefully in your hands.

Frameworks

There is no shortage of literature to consult in this space. In terms of classic texts, Geert Hofstede did pioneering work in the 1980s on culture, using the test ground of IBM. Edgar H. Schein's model[5] represents culture as a three-layered "lily pond", with espoused values and cultural artefacts underpinned by tacit cultural assumptions. Robert A. Cooke defined the widely respected Organisational Culture Inventory® (OCI®)[6].

Current good reads on culture are *"Who Moved My Cheese? An Amazing Way to Deal with Change in Your Work and in Your Life"*

---

[5] Schein, E.H. "Organizational Culture and Leadership", 5th ed., p25
[6] https://www.humansynergistics.com/change-solutions/change-solutions-for-organizations/assessments-for-organizations/organization-culture-inventory

by Spencer Johnson and *"Start with Why: How Great Leaders Inspire Everyone to Take Action"* by Simon Sinek.

More recently, in McKinsey Quarterly, in an article entitled *"Givers take all: The hidden dimension of corporate culture"* Adam Grant talked about how a culture of giving and reciprocity strengthened performance in the US intelligence services.[7]

Below are some diagnostics you can perform to determine your early approach to culture.

Diagnostic

How will you determine the culture of the organisation? By observation, discussion and reading. By looking at the tangible manifestations of culture. By asking employees why things are done the way they're done. By recognising inconsistencies between what's being said and what's being done.

When gauging whether action is needed on culture, one simple assessment involves looking at two dimensions—the strength of the culture and its positivity or negativity. This is similar to the Goffee and Jones model [8]which looks at "solidarity" and "sociability". Culture can be:

- **Strong.** A high degree of behavioural similarity exhibited by employees, even across different locations. A high degree of repeatable behaviour. There may seem to be an

[7] Grant, Adam. "Givers take all: The hidden dimension of corporate culture." *McKinsey Quarterly*, April 2013. Accessed May 19, 2017. http://www.mckinsey.com/business-functions/organization/our-insights/givers-take-all-the-hidden-dimension-of-corporate-culture.
[8] Schein, E.H. "Organizational Culture and Leadership", 5th ed.

invisible force guiding what needs to be done, without much obvious recourse to written policies and procedures—people just 'know' what needs to happen. Note, I have said nothing here about the culture being "nice" or "happy." Strength is a measure of how much the culture pervades the organisation. You can have a strong culture that is very tough.

- **Weak.** The opposite of the above. You get a variable impression as you visit and meet different parts of the organisation. Employee experience differs depending on what team they're in and their line manager. There is little to fall back on in the way of norms of behaviour—people have to "consult the policy". There is a sense of "herding kittens," as people act as individuals rather than conforming to a set of norms. It's hard to get cross-organisational work done successfully.

> Schein[9] says that the strength of a culture depends on (1) the length of time, (2) the stability of membership of the group, and (3) the emotional intensity of the actual historical learning experiences they've shared.

- **Positive.** Positive disposition towards the goals of the organisation. Generally good sentiments expressed towards and between employees—embracing diversity, empathy, respect, tolerance, and co-operation.
- **Negative.** Cynicism about the organisation. Signs of a lack of trust, siloes, protectionism, and defensiveness.

---

[9] Schein, E.H. "Organizational Culture and Leadership", 5th ed.

these moments and reflect hard on your response—chances are your response will set the scene for years to come.

A fascinating insight into culture comes from the book *"It's My Pleasure: The Impact of Extraordinary Talent and a Compelling Culture"* by Dee Ann Turner. Turner talks about the strong and distinct culture in the US chain of fried chicken restaurants, Chick-fil-A. As you read the book, you can sense how deeply Chick-fil-A's culture shapes its people. Customer service is a central tenet of their culture, so much so, they categorise their staff into either "the people serving the chicken" or "the people helping the people who serve the chicken." There are many gems in Turner's book, but I like the best the concept of **servant leadership**. When new employees join Chick-fil-A, at company events they get seated next to the CEO. Senior management offer their business class seats to junior staff members who might not otherwise ever fly club. Leaders go to the back of the line at lunchtime, talking and interacting with staff they encounter along the way. This fosters the sense that senior management wouldn't ask anything of new employees they haven't done themselves. There are lots of books about servant leadership, including *Leaders Eat Last: Why Some Teams Pull Together and Other Don't* by Simon Sinek and *Everybody Matters: The Extraordinary Power of Caring for Your People Like Family* by Bob Chapman and Raj Sisodia.

How to improve culture

Whichever situation you find yourself in, there are always steps you can take to improve the culture of the organisation. Here are the steps that have worked for me.

- **Management role modelling.** Change starts with self. How are you showing up every day? How about the executive team? Are they dedicated to the organisation's goals, even at the expense of their own objectives? Do they practice self-sacrifice? Do they collaborate? How engaged are they in the organisation? Why would you expect your staff to be any more engaged, or practice any better behaviours than the ones they see you model every day?
- **Staff engagement.** Talk to staff. Get under the skin of what motivates and what bothers them. Try to take early action to remove an irritating factor. It'll win you friends and show your staff that you're listening.
- **Communications.** Look at your staff communications. Are they authentic? Do they mirror the reality of employees' experience? Is the tone right?
- **Visual management.** What's important for the organisation to deliver? What is the strategy? Is it written up on the walls? Is it in sight when you make a coffee and reinforced around every corner? Is progress marked? Is success celebrated? In Save the Children, we put the strategy process up on a wall on huge posters, accompanied by two blackboards and lots of chalk so staff could actively engage with it.
- **History.** Dig back into the history of the organisation. What was its founding principle? Who were its founders? What values did they espouse? Is there something in the DNA of the organisation that can be emphasised? British Airways did this recently when it relaunched the historic motto 'To Fly, To Serve.' John Lewis has never deviated from its

motto 'Never knowingly undersold.' The founder of Save the Children, Eglantyne Jebb, was arrested in 1919 for demonstrating in the centre of London on behalf of starving children,[11] and there's a little of that rebellious spirit that still informs everything they do today.

- **Iconic moments**. As I mentioned before, sometimes a moment comes along that demands an action from you. You can't engineer it; you can't predict it. You also can't avoid it. You're presented with a dilemma, a decision, a problem, and the actions you take will send a message. A moment like this is an opportunity to set the tone in an incredibly powerful way. It's the thing people will talk about after you leave.

- **Little moments**. Conversely, there are hundreds of little moments that set the tone and say something about who you are and how you'd like the organisation to be. Everybody has a role to play in these. Someone once told me that culture is not something you can plan to implement—culture is being set in a thousand ways every day. The person you say hello to (as COO, always take the initiative and say hello), the door you hold open, the coffee you buy for someone in the line. Take every opportunity. People will notice.

- **Consistency**. Finally, reinforce the right messages every day, and ensure your team does as well. Day in and day out. Overtly and subtly, keep bolstering the new messages and the new behaviours. Staff will become anxious and

---

[11] Interestingly, when she was tried and fined £5, the prosecutor was so swayed by her argument, he paid the £5 himself

confused when they see unpredictable and contradictory messages – be reassuring and consistent.

---

12 mechanisms by which leaders embed their beliefs, values, and assumptions

Primary:

1. What they pay attention to, measure and control regularly
2. How they react to critical incidents and organizational crises
3. How they allocate resources
4. Role modelling, teaching, and coaching
5. How they allocate rewards and status
6. How they recruit, select, promote, and excommunicate

Secondary:

1. Organisational design and structure (see HR chapter)
2. Organisational systems and procedures (see IT and Operations chapters)
3. Rites and rituals of the organisation (see Communications and PR chapter)
4. Design of physical space, facades and buildings (see Facilities chapter)
5. Stories about important events and people (see Communications and PR chapter)

---

6. Formal statements of organisational philosophy, creeds, and charters (see Communications and PR chapter)

Source: Schein, E.H. "Organizational Culture and Leadership", 5th ed., p183

Dynamics of your senior management team

The team dynamic of your direct reports is essential to success. You want your team to function well, even when you're not in the room. You want their overall performance to be greater than the sum of their individual contributions. You want them motivated and engaged to help each other. To achieve this, you have to set a positive team dynamic by rewarding the behaviours you want to see. Get your team together and observe them.

- How well do they know each other?
- How do they work together?
- How do their working styles differ?
- Where are their natural affiliations?
- Where is there tension?
- Are they supporting each other?

Individually effective departments working in siloes will be dramatically less effective overall and will scupper your overall plans for the organisation. People don't have to be best friends, but they have to work together effectively. Look carefully. What are the problem areas where you can intervene? Where are the issues so intransigent that your only option is to replace somebody? Observe, consider, and decide. By the end of your first

100 days make whatever difficult decisions you need to make - if the team isn't going to work, face up to the difficult conversations.

Warning signs

You should be on the lookout for:

A **fragmented or weak culture**—different experiences for different people. Employees complaining that the overall organisational messages are not borne out in their experiences with their line managers.

No culture. I had a friend who joined a well-known financial services organisation. He was eagerly anticipating the role. I called him after his first day and asked him how it went, whom he met, what kind of induction he got, was the coffee any good, was there a canteen, etc. He said that he was just pointed to a desk and told to sit down. That was it. His new boss came over at some point and he got his instructions. This was not a junior role—it was a Director level position. During the time he was there, he never made a single friend. Extraordinary. He didn't stay long.

Good to great

If you already have a good culture to work with, then your life is going to be much easier and your role is to reinforce what you have. Culture is both big and small. It's shaped by iconic actions and key moments but also by the little things. A kind word, believing the best in someone, a genuine 'thank you'. Alternatively, an unkind comment, taking credit for the work of others, assigning blame - these little actions ripple out and get paid forward in multiples. Staff should never be told to wait for a new culture to be "rolled out". Aspirations can be set from the top, but it is what is borne out day to day by each and every staff member that is the real essence of culture. If a culture needs to be re-built or improved, there are certainly engagement programmes you can build and values you can adopt, but culture change always starts today.

10 questions to ask about Culture

1. What words would management use to describe the culture?
2. What words would staff use? Do they match?
3. What is the organisation's value set? Is it known? Is it authentic or just words on a wall?
4. Is the culture homogeneous, or does it vary across departments and geographies, and at different levels of seniority?
5. What is the history of the organisation? Has it grown organically or through acquisition? How long has the current management team been in place?
6. Who are the culture carriers in the organisation? These are the people who in challenging moments set the norms for how employees should react. They're often not on the executive team. Get to know them and get them on your side.
7. Is there a common sense of purpose in the organisation?
8. How do people wield influence in the organisation?
9. What do people say they like about the organisation? What do they dislike?
10. What do employee surveys tell you about the culture?

Further reading

Chapman, B. & Sisodia, R.: *"Everybody Matters: The Extraordinary Power of Caring for Your People Like Family"*

Needle, D.: "Business in Context: An Introduction to Business and Its Environment"

Sinek, S.: "Leaders Eat Last: Why Some Teams Pull Together and Others Don't"Sinek, S.: "Start with Why: How Great Leaders Inspire Everyone to Take Action"

Schein, E.: *"Organizational Culture and Leadership"*

Turner, D.: *"It's My Pleasure: The Impact of Extraordinary Talent and a Compelling Culture"*

"How to Change Your Organization's Culture." *Wall Street Journal*

"Givers take all: The Hidden dimension of corporate culture." *McKinsey Quarterly*

3. STRATEGY

You have presumably taken on the position of COO, either because you believe that the organisation has a compelling strategy, or because it's willing to work with you to create one. Your most important responsibility is to ensure that your organisation has:

- assessed itself and its changing environment;
- correctly identified its purpose;
- analysed the most significant challenges to achieving its purpose;
- defined the correct and implementable actions to address them.

If not, all the work you and your employees will do isn't going to take your organisation in the right direction.

What is strategy?

I define strategy as answers to the following three critical questions:

1. The overall objective—the "Why" of the organisation. Why does it exist? What's its mission?
2. The strategy—the "What" of the organisation. What does it need to do to succeed?
3. The goals—the "How" of the organization. How will the organisation achieve its strategy?

While most organisations have a strategy written down, how many of these are a genuine blueprint for success? A good strategy is underpinned by what the organisation is truly about. It's clear about what the organisation is *not* - it provides a framework for ruling *out* courses of action. It resonates with what every person in the organisation is doing. If employees can't see a clear line between their day job and the end game, their motivation and focus will suffer.

Conversely, when the strategy is strong, there is an invisible thread pulling you and all your people towards your goal. Everything hangs off it: projects, finances, operational plans. A strong strategy is the framework that the rest of this book hangs off. It puts guardrails around finance and budgets, people and talent plans, procurement and risk management. Everything each department does must start with strategy.

The link between strategy and culture

According to Schein[12], "one of the most central elements of any culture is the assumptions the members of the organization share about their identity and ultimate mission or functions. These are not necessarily very conscious but can surface if one probes the strategic decisions that the organization makes." In other words, strategy and culture are fundamentally interlinked. The work you do as a COO on strategy must take into account the culture within which it's located.

Frameworks

Thousands of books have been written about strategy. One superb catch-all book that contains detailed guides and tools on

---

[12] Schein, E.H. "Organizational Culture and Leadership", 5th ed.

setting strategy is *"The Strategy Book"* by Max McKeown. Another great book is *"Good Strategy Bad Strategy: The Difference and Why It Matters"* by Richard Rumelt. Rumelt has been described as the "strategist's strategist." In his book, he provides a comprehensive analysis of what strategy is and what it's not. In particular, I have noted five key points he makes on strategy:

1. **Simplicity.** "The core of strategy work is always the same: discovering the critical factors in a situation and designing a way of co-ordinating and focusing actions to deal with those factors".

2. **Challenges.** "A good strategy does more than urge us forward toward a goal or vision. A good strategy honestly acknowledges the challenges being faced and provides an approach to overcoming them."

3. **Strengths.** "The most basic idea of strategy is the application of strength against weakness. Or, if you prefer, strength applied to the most promising opportunity."

4. **Implementable.** "A strategy that fails to define a variety of plausible and feasible immediate actions is missing a critical component". Strategy "builds a bridge between the challenge and action, between desire and immediate objectives that lie within grasp."

5. **A filter to stop doing things.** "Good strategy requires leaders who are willing and able to say *no* to a wide variety of actions and interests. Strategy is as much about what an organisation does not do, as it is about what it does."

Diagnostic: How strong is the organisation's strategy?

So, how can you tell whether you have a strong strategy, and what are some signs of a weak one?

Let's get back to basics. McKeown distils strategy down to five questions[13]. In order to be complete, a strategy needs to be able to answer these questions:

- Where are we?
- Where do we want to go?
- What changes have to be made?
- How should changes be made?
- How shall we measure progress?

A strategy that doesn't answer the above questions clearly is not going to be comprehensive.

Next, you need to consider whether the strategy is effective. Is it:

- Sufficiently distinct and unique? Does it hone down your organisation's offering to a unique selling point?
- Clear? Steve Jobs once said that the ultimate sophistication is simplicity. Is it defined well-enough to hang the entire organisational architecture on it?
- A source of competitive advantage? Taking into account the environment, strengths of the organisation, competitive landscape, market forces, is this the path that

---

[13] McKeown, Max. *The Strategy Book: How to Think and Act Strategically to Deliver Outstanding Results*. FT Press, 2016.

is going to light the way for the organisation to move from strength to strength?

- Implementable? Is it sufficiently grounded in reality and in the inherent capabilities of the organisation to be able to be brought to fruition?

As COO, you can find the answers to these questions as follows:

1. Ask, discuss, probe. Speak to the Board of Directors, the Executive team, middle management and staff. Can they articulate the strategy to you, and their role in implementing it?
2. Benchmark. Look at what competitors are doing. Look at what organisations you admire are doing. Does your organisation's strategy stand up?
3. Look externally. What are the drivers moving the market today and the ones that will impact the market tomorrow?
4. Look internally. Where is the energy in the organisation? Where is capability developing quickly? What does the organisation do well? What can be pivoted into new offerings?

As COO, you must get the strategy right. If the organisation you joined already has a strong strategy, you can get straight to execution. If the strategy is weak, your priority is to re-define it. And if the strategy is fundamentally wrong, and the organisation isn't willing to change it, then you can still make things better, department by department, using the diagnostics and the frameworks in this book. Set yourself a time period (say, two years) and a set number of things that you can improve tangibly. Work diligently on getting those things fixed, but recognise that your impact will only go so far and you may not want to stay in this role long term.

If you have to create a new strategy

If you conclude that the organisation needs a new strategy, this is going to be your priority in your first 100 days. It will involve significant effort from you at the expense of other priorities. However, it does mean you get to play a pivotal role in helping define the organisation's trajectory for the future.

Vast tomes have been written about defining strategy, from Porter to Drucker, from Six Sigma techniques to Blue Ocean. This book cannot do justice to all these in a short space, but I'll give you two outlines: one for a traditional approach and one for a more disruptive one.

Classic strategy development

Most approaches to strategy generally follow a similar process, which involves:

1. Looking outside—at the market, at what's moving, and at the key environmental forces that will shape your sector in the future. The much-used PESTLE tool (Political, Economic, Social, Technical, Legal and Environmental) is still a useful framework here, as is Porter's five forces model.
2. Looking inside—at the internal capabilities of the organisation, at its unique attributes, and at what it does better than anyone else. The SWOT (Strengths,

Weaknesses, Opportunities, Threats) is the traditional tool of choice here. One of the most dramatic and successful examples of understanding the core capabilities of an organisation is how Steve Jobs refocused Apple on a drastically reduced product set when he returned to the organisation. Porter's Value Chain analysis is also a useful tool for the COO.

3. Prioritising goals and setting a path. Given the above two analyses, what are going to be the key strategies for the organisation to overcome its challenges and capitalise on its opportunities? Often this can start with a long list that is then distilled into a shortlist of strategies that will yield the most success.

4. Defining how the organisation will get there. Once you establish the "What," outline "How" you'll get there and what is needed in terms of talent, technology, and other resources.

5. Setting the definitions of success and how they'll be measured. How will the organisation know it's moving in the right direction? What measures will either validate this, or alert management to problems?

Strategy for disruption

If the organisation is seeking new markets and trying to create something truly new, it needs to think creatively. The much lauded disruptors of recent years, such as Airbnb and Uber are so admired because they entered what appeared to be saturated market space (hotels and taxis, respectively) and used technology to disintermediate and create cheaper and more convenient offerings, getting right in the way of existing, long-established players. In their book *"Blue Ocean Strategy: How to Create Uncontested Market Space and Make the Competition Irrelevant"*, W. Chan Kim and Renee Mauborgne outline six "paths" to reconstructing market boundaries and creating "uncontested market space":

Path 1: "Look across alternative industries" for inspiration. Consider the end user and what their alternatives are to your offering. Is there an offering in between the two that can be created? They give the example of cinemas and restaurants - not aligned from a sector perspective, but genuine alternatives for the consumer.

Path 2: "Look across strategic groups within industries". Within each given industry sector a different strategic group exists with its own prices and performance points. Understanding what causes customers to trade up or down within this value set can create opportunities for new offerings.

Path 3: "Look across the chain of buyers". The authors distinguish between buyers, users and influencers. Challenging who you are really selling to can yield insights.

Path 4: "Look across complementary product and service offerings". Taking the customers' point of view and seeing the associations between different offerings can suggest new pairings that were previously not obvious.

Path 5: "Look across functional or emotional appeal to buyers". Some products are more utilitarian, others have a more emotional appeal. Dialling up or down these characteristics and challenging the perceptions of a product can alter its appeal. Look at how Kindle advertised its device, alongside breakfast cereal and dogs, to position it as a much loved family item. Or look at how the Irish tourist board took a stretch of road and branded it the Wild Atlantic Way, using stunning photography to illustrate its appeal.

Path 6: "Look across time". Find the decisive, observable trends that are going to shape the future for your organisation, take them to their logical conclusion and iterate the organisation's offering accordingly.

Tips for success

Regardless of what combination of methodologies you decide to use, these 12 techniques will help you to successfully create a new strategy:

1. Be **realistic** about the effort this is going to take. What will it mean for your first 100 days? Manage expectations that you may not be as visible as you'd like— it may take longer for you to assume some operational responsibilities. Lean on the talents of your senior team and entrust the day job to them.

2. Involve the **Executive team**. They need to appreciate the need to review the strategy. They need to understand that strategy changes will have consequences for them and

their teams. They need to know that they're part of a greater whole and will have to make sacrifices for the greater good of the organisation.

3. Allow time for proper **thinking**. Real, deep, complex thought. This needs to take place alone, as well as with your CEO and with the leadership team. Resist the urge to just get on and deliver something. According to McKeown, "strategists who don't take time to think are just planners." Some of the most successful strategic shifts— from Apple to Uber—have been in the creation of a new category, a new product, or a pivot on an existing offering or service. These are unlikely to arise in a crunched one-hour-long meeting sandwiched between other meetings. Take your time. Take your people away from their normal location and spend a few days thinking.

4. Source your inputs from as **diverse** a range of sectors and organisations as possible. Often, the kernel of a great new idea is joining two concepts that haven't been previously considered.

5. **Embrace the discomfort**. It's only when people are feeling the discomfort that you are getting somewhere. A HR professional I once met talked of the importance of the "passionate unfiltered debate." There has to be enough trust and familiarity in the room for the senior team to really go at it—to expose the issues and to debate the trade-offs.

6. Be **pragmatic and dispassionate**. Realise that not everyone on the team may survive the launch of the new strategy.

7. Involve **middle management.** They often know the organisation best and will be critical to the implementation of the new strategy and to the engagement of the general staff.

8. **Communicate** with your people. Don't gild the lily. If tough changes are coming, say so.

9. Open up a **conversation**. At all levels and across all divisions, foster a willingness and an openness to discuss external shifts and what they will mean for your organisation. Refer to staff dialogue often in your presentations to staff and encourage them to reach across siloes to continue the conversation.

10. Push to the **extremes,** then work back. When modelling the impact of future factors, exaggerate the drivers and see what happens. For example, apply the impacts of digital technology to your organisational model in an extreme sense and model the effects. Then work back to a more realistic assessment.

11. Be **realistic** about how much change can be effected at once. If over the course of 2-3 years you succeed in dislodging 2-3 deeply entrenched problems or issues, you've done extremely well. This is a marathon, not a sprint.

12. Treat a new strategy as a starting point for a *new approach* to strategy. Map out how and when the new strategy will be revisited. Little and often is good, compounded with deeper reviews quarterly and annually. Nourish and feed the strategic thinking process. Make it less intimidating to engage with by making it a habit. Like regularly going to

the gym, build up the muscle memory of looking up from the day-to-day to ensure you're still going in the right direction.

Suggested outline of a strategy document

Once you have devised the strategy, you'll need to explain it to the organisation by writing a strategy document. Below are the key elements it should contain:

- Where the organisation has come from
- The successes it has achieved thus far
- The changing environment and context in which it operates
- The vision for the future
- The unique role that the organisation plays
- The specific strategies that will get it there
- The timelines
- The challenges
- How you'll measure success
- The role the organisation's people play
- The role of the support functions

Implementing the strategy. Execution – strategy into action

Once the organisation has set the right strategy, the role of the COO is to put it into action. This requires a practical, execution-focused mind set. It requires the ability to translate lofty concepts into real actions. What are you going to do first? People need an action plan that they can understand and implement.

Making the link between strategy and action are **goals**, underpinned by a change process. Goals must fulfil the description of "x to y by z." That is, they must take account where you currently are, where you want to get to, and the timeline to do so.

Connective tissue

Goals and detailed plans form the connective tissue between the strategy of the organisation and the action of here and now. It's an essential translation service. It's important to ensure there is rigour, coherence and connectivity between where the organisation wants to go and its actions. I've often uncovered non-sequitur types of action, along the lines of "We need to offer our customers a better experience - so we have to buy this system." There must be a clear line of sight as to how a particular goal is going to reinforce the strategy you have so painstakingly put together.

Goals must connect strategy and action, but also functions and departments. This is where execution often breaks down. In the Harvard Business Review article "Why Strategy Execution Unravels – and What to Do About It," the authors bust five myths about the execution of strategy:[14]

Myth 1: Execution equals alignment. In many cases the problem is not the lack of SMART objectives or measures of success, it's the

---

[14] Sull, Donald, Rebecca Homkes, and Charles Sull. "Why Strategy Execution Unravels – and What to Do About It." *Harvard Business Review*, March 2015. Accessed May 22, 2017. https://hbr.org/2015/03/why-strategy-execution-unravelsand-what-to-do-about-it.

fact that departments don't operate cohesively towards the given goal. Something in the interconnectivity between functions can break down and undermine execution.

Myth 2: Execution means sticking to the plan. On the contrary, in this rapidly moving environment agility and the ability to capitalise on opportunities and to react to problems are highly prized. McKeown reinforces this when he says that reacting and responding to events is just as important as planning.

Myth 3: Communication equals understanding. Management often assumes that staff properly understand the strategy and its connection to business plans, because they've been regularly communicated to staff. Research shows that not to be the case. Staff can become incredibly confused by a mix of multiple messages. The strategy has to be simple, and has to be repeated often, for everyone to be on the same page.

Myth 4: A performance culture drives execution. Of course, a focus on performance is important. However, done excessively, and at the expense of other attributes such as teamwork and agility, it can drive the wrong behaviours.

Myth 5: Execution should be driven from the top. You, the CEO and the executive team play a key role in execution. However, when you push execution from the top without engaging middle management, it can create a dependency culture where middle management doesn't feel confident in handling matters. This can cause major problems with succession when a leader moves on. Far more enduring is the model of "distributed management' where the strategy is owned, and driven, by a cohort across the organisation.

This, in essence, is the recipe for strategy. If you know "Why" the organisation does what it does, "What" it needs to do to succeed, and "How" it's going to do it, then you have strong building blocks for success. All you need now is an excellent change management process. This is the subject of the next chapter.

Warning signs

Rumelt says that "bad strategy is the active avoidance of the hard work of crafting a good strategy." Alastair Campbell[15] says "the problem is that, in most situations, we tend not to strive for this clarity of thought." A big warning sign for you should be a **woolly, aspirational, unclear, all-embracing strategy**.

Another sign is an organisation that is **constantly on high alert**, flipping between new ideas and crisis management, and changing course constantly. As Michael Porter says[16], "an organisation without a strategy is willing to try anything."

A strategy that is **lip service only** – written, put on a wall or on a shelf and not dusted off again for another three years when it's time to revise it.

A strategy that is **all things to all people** – there's something in there for everyone, and management hasn't been sufficiently discerning or courageous to say "No" to vested interests. A good strategy has hard choices embedded in it. If everyone is happy

---

[15] Campbell, Alastair *"Winners and how they succeed"*
[16] Campbell, Alastair *"Winners and how they succeed"*

with the strategy, it probably means not enough choices have been made.

A strategy that's just "**work harder and achieve more**," even if wrapped up to look good. As Richard Rumelt says, "simply being ambitious is not a strategy."

A strategy that doesn't take into account the **changing environment** and the possibility that the organisation's core model and value proposition might be disrupted.

A strategy that **staff don't understand.**

A strategy that is **fluff** – "We wish to be the most admired ... in the industry" type strategy. Really, the most admired? Just get yourself a good PR team then and be done with it.

Ten questions to ask about strategy:

Strategy design

1. What problems are your organisation and your strategy trying to solve?
2. How has the strategy come about? Who was involved in setting it? What were the considerations behind the new strategy?
3. Does the strategy set a clear enough direction to allow you to exclude or cut out certain business lines or activities?
4. What are the drivers that are shaping the future of the organisation?
5. What is going to disrupt the organisation's model?

6. What are the drivers of income? Are they in balance? Are they diversified? Where is the growth?
7. Are there activities that are crying out to be centralised, outsourced or stopped altogether?

Strategy implementation

1. Does the organisation have the talent it requires to get itself there?
2. Is the employee value proposition strong enough to attract the talent it requires?
3. How are the Technology and Operations platforms? Are the technical enablers there to facilitate progress?

Further reading

Campbell, A.: *"Winners: And How They Succeed"*

Kim, W.C., Mauborgne, R.: *"Blue Ocean Strategy: How to Create Uncontested Market Space and Make Competition Irrelevant"*

McKeown, M.: *"The Strategy Book"*

Rumelt, R.: *"Good Strategy Bad Strategy: The Difference and Why It Matters"*

Sull, D., Homkes, R. & Sull, C.,: "*Why Strategy Execution Unravels – and What to Do About It.*" *Harvard Business Review*, March 2015

4. Change

Change is the alchemy, the metamorphosis that turns a well-designed strategy into reality. A change capability is the third fundamental pillar of a successful framework for the COO. After all the work in the last chapter to set or revise the strategy, now you have to implement it. All strategy is for nought unless it's translated into reality via a change process.

Even if the organisation isn't going through a major strategic change, as a COO you're almost always accountable for leading a change agenda. Whether it's in response to a crisis, industry movements, or disruption, you almost always have the frequently unpopular task of initiating and leading transformation. Furthermore, at the COO level change is almost always fundamental in nature – to culture, product sets, ways of working – the things that people typically care most about and respond to emotionally.

Manage this process well, and you'll see a sustainable legacy come to life – a shift of the organisation in the direction of its overall goals. Get it wrong, and all the good theory will never become practice.

What is change all about?

A well-honed change capability is about the openness and the responsiveness of your organisation in embracing changes that will propel it forward. You can have a successful delivery, for example of a technology system, but with inadequate change management it won't be accepted and the benefits won't be realised. Later in the book, I give an example of a facilities change I spearheaded which, while delivering on the tangible goals, did not achieve all it could because we didn't focus sufficiently on the change management aspects.

Changes are often about finding efficiency. As COO you are uniquely placed to spot these opportunities. You have a better view than perhaps anyone, even the CEO, of all the departments that make up the organisation and how they operate end to end. You have the unique perspective on what parts of the ecosystem light up when certain processes take place, where the bottlenecks are, where investment is needed, and what areas aren't pulling their weight.

Whatever the reason, change is much more about people's psychology and emotions than it is about tasks. To preside over a successful change agenda, you need to find out how to influence, motivate and inspire people in your organisation. You need a profound belief in the merits of the changes. You need confidence and tenacity to see them through, however tough the journey may be. Finally, you need patience – change is hard and takes time.

culture, corporate change management has
ure against it. John P. Kotter defined an eight-
hange management[17]. Those stages are:

1. Establish a sense of **urgency**. If people are going to accept the disruption associated with change, they need to understand why it's necessary, and why now.
2. Create **coalition**. Who are going to be the key operators to lead this change?
3. Develop the **vision**. Envision what the future could look like if the change took place.
4. **Communicate** the vision. Share this with people to engage them.
5. **Empower people**. Quite simply, give them the tools and the resources they need to be successful.
6. **Secure short term wins**. The motivational and galvanising impact of early success is huge.
7. **Consolidate** and move forward. Build on the early wins to maintain momentum.
8. **Anchor** the change. Once change is achieved, put those markers in the sand to prevent them from regressing.

Target Operating Model

A useful framework to translate strategy into realisable business plans is to use the lens of the target operating model. Your

---

[17] Kotter, John P. *https://www.kotterinternational.com/8-steps-process-for-leading-change/*

people, processes, technology and organisational structure must align behind what the organisation is trying to achieve.

A popular operating model is the McKinsey (Peters, Athos and Waterman) "7S" operating model[18]:

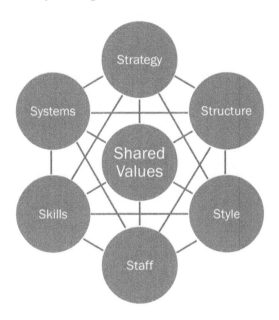

It portrays the different elements of an organisation that must be working together for the change to take effect. It poses questions such as - Do the values underpin the strategy? Are staff, structure and systems set up to reinforce success or to sabotage it? Is management style in line with its values? Are there the right skills inside the organisation? Use this model to check how all-embracing your change programmes are. Are these different elements coming together in a mutually supportive and congruent way, or are some running against what you're trying to achieve?

---

[18] Accessed from "The Strategy Book", McKeown, M., 2nd ed., 2016

How effective is change management in your organisation?

In order to gauge whether your organisation has the ability to successfully deliver change, you'll need to establish the following:

- Whether the right change projects are being incepted, i.e., whether the scarce resources of the organisation are focused on fixing the right problems. By "resources", I mean time and money of course, but I also count the *energy* of your people as a highly scarce and valuable resource. Are they suffering change fatigue?
- Whether the problems are well-enough defined.
- Whether solutions are being thought about in the broadest sense, and whether the right ones are chosen for the right reasons.
- Whether solutions are delivered on time and within budget more often than not.
- Whether changes are accepted by the organisation or are suffering from "tissue rejection".
- Whether the organisation is evolving through each change, harnessing good practice, learning from mistakes and moving up the maturity curve, or whether it's making the same mistakes over and over again.

How to find out? Ask people about the major changes they've observed over the past 2-3 years, how they think those changes have landed, and whether they're feeling confident about the current changes. Look objectively at the change portfolio and see if you think it's achievable.

Your role as COO in overseeing change

Here are some tips on how you can lead from the front:

- **Start with the strategy.** If the strategy is good, the compelling arguments for change will be embedded in it. If your organisation is engaging in major change initiatives that don't link to the strategy, you need to ask why. Valid reasons include mandatory regulatory or compliance requirements (which have dominated the banking industry for the past decade) and mandatory technology upgrades (where systems will fall apart unless addressed). However, even while working on these, teams can make incremental improvements along the way. When compliance demands are so onerous that there is little or no "discretionary" budget left over, maximise the benefit of each intervention. If you have the patient open on the table already, it's possible to use the opportunity to make other improvements.

- **Push and pull factors.** Be upfront with people about the "Why." Sometimes the "Why" is about seizing a wonderful, game-changing new opportunity. Sometimes it's about doing something that has to be done. Your job is to grasp one or two really big, nasty nettles and deal with them. If you want to leave your organisation in a better state than how you found it, you have to drive a balance between the quick wins that garner support and the big, fundamental improvements from which future generations will benefit.

If you get people engaged in the "Why", everything else becomes easier. Don't unnecessarily deplete your personal reserves of goodwill and influence by pushing a project. People should be engaging in the project because they see its inherent benefits, not because the COO says so. There will be times when you'll just have to muscle a project through using your political capital. However, it's draining for you and will deplete your goodwill, so use sparingly.

- **If it's unglamorous and difficult, say so**. Don't be afraid to tell things as they are – people know it anyway and will respect your honesty in not sugar-coating it. You can reward the drudgery by regular shout-outs and updates, keeping motivation up and the end game in sight.

- **Build a cohort at all levels**. Don't make the mistake of focusing only on top management. Find the subject matter experts and the culture carriers, and keep the channels open with them. The culture carriers will give you the word on the street and will carry a lot more people in the middle ranks with them than you ever will. Respect these people, give them your time, and they'll repay you with interest. Plus, you'll pick up a lot of useful information along the way.

- **Be prepared to flex and to give things up**. If an aspect of a project you're championing isn't working or is proving unpopular, be humble enough to amend it or to give it up entirely. You'll demonstrate your willingness to listen and respond. This will motivate and inspire people.

- **Ensure that projects end properly**. Mark all successes, assess them for benefits and for lessons learned, and then celebrate. This is huge. Failure to acknowledge success and mark completion can lead to a sense of relentlessness and pointlessness. It's exhausting. You must put a punctuation mark at the end of every project – say it's finished and congratulate all involved.

You also need to commercially challenge the incremental benefits of a project's successive phases. Often, 80% of the benefits of projects take place in the early stages, with diminishing returns after that. Later stages of the same project should be evaluated and prioritised alongside newer projects, which may deliver more benefit for the organisation. Grouping together pet projects under the umbrella of another one is a common trick used by political agents – don't let your organisation fall for it.

Knowing how to get things done

Before I became a COO, I held two different Chief of Staff roles. I had been in my organisation five years when I got my first Chief of Staff role, ten years in my second. I truly believe that the single most important skill for a Chief of Staff (and, to almost the same extent, for a COO), is knowing how to get things done in an organisation. This entails knowing whom to call and for what, but more importantly, it requires deep relationships with people whom you can call on in times of need. No matter how large your organisation, you can develop networks so that you're never more than a few degrees of separation away from finding the right person for a particular issue.

If you've been hired from outside the organisation, you won't have immediate access to these networks. Get yourself a knowledgeable assistant or a Chief of Staff who knows the people and their sensitivities, and who can smooth the pathways and open doors. Build on that by investing in the key relationships that you'll need to be successful.

Discipline

At the root of all good execution is discipline – being confident in the benefit of a particular change programme and not wavering. Organisations that pursue a small number of changes with relentless focus, tenacity and dogged determination while avoiding distractions along the way, will always be more successful than those who waver.

The following passage from *Winners: And How They Succeed* by Alastair Campbell characterises the distracted leader. Read it and see if it reminds you of a current world leader:

> "Too obsessed with day-to-day coverage, too easily blown off track by day-to-day events, they have a tendency to flit from issue to issue, rarely engaging with them fully and rarely joining up their various responses into a considered overall approach."

I find that COOs tend to be disciplined people by nature. Instil this sense of discipline when overseeing change management.

> **Case study – a common architecture**
>
> At Save the Children we have a federated global model, which means that each member country has autonomy over its fundraising and infrastructure budget, as long as it makes the appropriate contributions to our central international programming team. This has its advantages, but it can also lead to a lack of coherence around IT strategy and architecture choices. In the UK, we were looking at a new digital platform to improve engagement with our supporters. The US was doing the same. I reached out to my counterpart in the US and said, "Whatever we choose, we have to do this together." He agreed, and from that moment the architecture of the digital platforms of the two biggest members of our global movement was fused. I hope we've made life better for the organisation for years to come. That's what legacy is all about.

Project portfolio management

As COO, you'll rarely be involved in the details of individual projects. Your role is ensuring good governance over the organisation's change portfolio. A frequent mistake made - even by large, sophisticated organisations - is to have a loose attitude toward incepting new projects without due regard for the capacity of the organisation. This is a frequent, and serious, impediment to effectiveness. Your Head of Change / Programme Management Office needs to have the mandate to assess the suite of change projects that are underway. Your Executive team needs to have the necessary discipline to choose their change agenda judiciously. This is important for multiple reasons:

- Too much change will limit the overall effectiveness of the projects already underway, exhaust and deplete your people and lead to change fatigue. If you have a hundred projects on the go, often with the same key staff responsible for landing them, you will inch forward on all of them, rather than make great strides on a few.

- Often, business stakeholders have no idea how much is actually underway on their behalf. They don't see the bigger picture of delivery and then complain when their work isn't prioritised.

Visibility of change

In Barclays Wealth, I was asked to analyse all the change initiatives our department was making on behalf of the Private Bank. Once my team itemised what was actually in flight, people were astounded to

learn that there were 120 discrete change initiatives underway. We analysed them according to effort, funding and project stage, then grouped them by stakeholder. We then used this information to get the front office teams to prioritise what they wanted to take place, and reported back to them regularly on the progress of their chosen projects. If they chose to jump mid-stream from one project to another, we showed them the cost, the delay and the waste this caused. The clarity and the visibility this exercise achieved was game-changing.

Two of the greatest gifts you can give your organisation are clarity of strategy and an environment conducive to operational excellence. Cleaning up the change portfolio, sequencing things instead of doing them all at once, and closing down legacy projects will free up your talented people to deliver. It will release and supercharge your organisation. Staff will appreciate regaining the ability to do a good job – nobody likes being forced to do a hundred things at once and doing them badly. Most people want to deliver something of quality. They derive satisfaction from that – give them back that gift.

Supporting the delivery life cycle

All change, whether implemented traditionally or in a more agile way, goes through a life cycle. The COO has a particular role to play at each stage.

If you were formerly a Programme Management Officer (a very good training ground for COOs), you'll be familiar with the concepts and the stages below. Ironically, you may struggle more than most with adjusting to your new role. Schulte says[19], "A significant challenge to the project manager is when and how to intervene but, for the most part, as they say, just 'let them play' ... Recognise that it is your coaching... which minimises your need to be the referee too." The following section talks through the major stages of a change programme and what you should be watching out for.

1) Initiation

At this point, Management grants a project initial approval to proceed. The project team will define the user needs, forecast

---

[19] "Complex IT Project Management: 16 Steps to Success", Schulte P.

benefits, develop proofs of concept, and assess feasibility. Importantly, Management will appoint the "sponsor" for the project. This may be you or another member of the Executive team. The sponsor is saying that:

- They support this project
- They want it to happen
- They will use their personal and political capital to make a success of it
- They believe in the benefits of the project
- They believe this is the right project to deliver the benefits
- They're comfortable with the resources at hand (money, people, technology, support, change capability) to make the project a success
- They're willing to put their name and their reputation on the line to get the project done

A long time ago in Barclays, we had "Promise keepers" – a group of senior people who made sure the must-do projects in the organisation got done. They could select only ten projects in any one year. If all else failed, these projects would get implemented – and others could fall by the wayside or be delayed if necessary. We moved away from this accountability system over the years, but I always liked the simplicity and purpose behind it.

The project sponsor should agree with the statements above and be prepared to forego other initiatives until this one is done. By ensuring this commitment, you'll help your organisation draw a golden thread between its objective, its strategy, and its change agenda. Cutting projects that don't meet this threshold will save your organisation untold heartache down the line. Remember, strategy is as much about what you *don't* do as it's about what you do.

Be the voice of realism. Impatient for results, people tend to be over-optimistic in projecting timelines and benefits. There is little incentive for people to consider the full, lifetime cost of the project. Push for this – be the voice of realism. You'll encourage the organisation to mature in its assessment of change.

2) Design

Once the project enters the design phase, the COO should encourage stakeholders to keep sight of the end goal. Any project must start with a problem, not a solution. It's a common mistake for business stakeholders to jump at the newest technology as a panacea to all their problems, either because they've been dazzled by a sales pitch or because another organisation has acquired the latest technology. Intervene and advocate for the proper consideration of the core issues and a reasoned evaluation of the possible solutions. This may lead to a less glamorous solution, but ultimately, a more suitable and affordable one.

If your technology team has an in-house development capability and open source platforms, they may be able to create a proof of concept of the solution in a very short time. Your business users will get to make mistakes on an inexpensive prototype before committing to a multi-million-pound system and expensive contractors.

Support your Supply Chain team in performing good market research and appropriate tendering procedures. It doesn't have to take months to do, and will save money over time. Challenge your Technology and Supply Chain teams to be as expedient as possible, but also stand up for them and for the rigour of their processes.

3) Development

During development, the project often goes quiet, and motivation can suffer. To keep the motivation levels up give shout outs (and doughnuts) to the team – mark small wins, and keep people focused on the end game. If business users intervene with a new set of demands, encourage them to really consider whether they are required at this point. It is often more effective to get the current stage of development done and add further functionality later. Only if there is a change in circumstance that requires the project to back up, should you allow it to go into reverse. Because that's what happens – you can't just throw in a few more requirements. You'll need to return to the design stage.

4) Test

This is an area where as Sponsor and/or COO, you get to flex your muscle. To foster acceptance and to ensure people get the product they asked for, get it tested it as widely as possible. This is where you call in favours and engage the best people. Inevitably, when the first round of testing produces issues and defects, you'll need to be the voice of reason and the moderator to distinguish between drop-dead issues and niggles, and to keep people focused on getting the project launched.

5) Implementation

The project is launching! Mark the moment and congratulate the teams. Prepare people for the inevitable bumpiness that will come with the launch, beg their indulgence and patience. Be available to the team to support them through the nerves and the drama. Be human and empathetic – if people are going above and beyond their direct responsibilities, working round the clock and on weekends to get things done, recognise it and call it out (while not wishing to make a habit of this!). Buy everyone drinks.

6) Post-implementation review

Promoting accountability is an important element of the COO role. This is the most thoughtful and neglected part of the project life cycle, and yet one that's most important from a Board and Executive standpoint. Was it all worthwhile? Did it achieve what the organisation set out to do? What did the teams learn? What will they never do again? What was really good and needs to be systematised and harnessed for the future? For major programmes, it can fall to you to do this – make it fun and motivational. It can be done offsite as part of the post-implementation celebration. Spend 45 minutes capturing insights before heading out for dinner. Make the time for this – it's important. Neglect it, and you'll throw away one of the best learning opportunities your organisation can get.

Warning signs

Below are signs that indicate your organisation does not have a well-flexed change "muscle." This will hamper all change efforts and impact success.

- Projects that spin out and out forever, with no closure and few checkpoints along the way
- Change fatigue in the organisation
- A history of failed projects
- A lack of awareness of whether projects have achieved their forecasted benefits
- An overwhelming array of projects
- A theoretical list of "priority" projects not borne out by reality and lots more pet projects underway
- Demotivated and harassed project teams
- Lack of clear budgets assigned to projects, often accompanied with macho "we'll just work harder" attitude. This is not working smart and it's hampering the organisation's ability to deliver what matters. People are not computers – they don't multi-task well. Asking them to drive forward a confusing array of initiatives is locking up their potential, burning valuable energy, hampering productivity and making your leadership team look bad.

Ten questions to ask about Change Management

1. What is the staff's attitude towards change? What is their experience of it?
2. What is the change capability within the organisation – both in project teams and among the staff?

3. What are the most recent changes in the organisation? How have they landed?
4. Does management accept change management as something that needs to be taken into consideration, or is project success just assumed?
5. How much change has the organisation been through in recent years?
6. Who leads the change in the organisation? Is it viewed as solely led by management, or is it federated and staff-initiated?
7. What is the governance around the change portfolio and around incepting new projects?
8. Do projects generally get implemented on time and on budget? If not, what lessons have been learned?
9. What must-do projects have been implemented this year? Were they appropriately resourced?
10. Is there a clear line of sight between the strategy and the change portfolio?

Further reading

Rowland, D. & Higgs, M.: "Sustaining Change: Leadership That Works"

Schulte, P.: "Complex IT Project Management: 16 Steps to Success"

Kotter, P.: "Leading Change", Harvard Business Review, 1995

Bridges, S.; *Making Transitions: Making the Most of Change*

Section 2: Technical areas

So, you are prepared, mentally and physically, for your role. You have a sense of the culture of the organisation. You know how much work needs to be done on the strategy. You have a plan to turn it into a reality via a change programme.

You now need to gauge the technical areas under your responsibility. You need a diagnostic of each department, to assess their strengths and areas for development. Doing this will shape your priorities for the year ahead and help you determine who is performing strongly, and where certain areas need strengthening.

Very few COOs come to their new roles as experts in all fields. As long as you're aware of your strengths and weaknesses, and you consider them in the team that you hire around you, this is perfectly normal. However, you must resist the temptation to over-involve yourself in your preferred areas or to neglect those that you're less comfortable with. Avoid these classic errors.

Risks of being hands-off in the areas you understand less

- Your department head may misinterpret this as lack of interest
- Staff will notice and be de-motivated
- After you lose your new person status, asking "newbie" questions will be harder
- When something goes wrong, you'll have little or no relationships on which to fall back and will come across as ill-informed

Risks of over-involving yourself in your pet areas

- You'll frustrate your department head
- You'll undermine your department head in front of others, which will weaken their position
- It may be mistaken for a lack of trust in the expertise of your department head
- You'll get overly drawn into operational details
- The department will become less decisive due to you hampering the decision-making

Once you have completed the diagnostics in this book, you can determine the areas that need more or less time, attention, funding and energy from you. You'll do it on the basis of an objective assessment rather than on the basis of your personal comfort levels.

General questions to ask

In addition to asking your department heads the technical questions, ask them how much time they're spending on relationships and people. What is the quality of the relationships they have fostered? Which members of the Board do they align with? What is their relationship with the CEO? How do they build their teams? How do they attract and retain talent? Who do they align with in their peer groups?

Here are some good opening questions to ask your department heads, to build a picture of how their departments are doing. Take them on board and supplement with the detailed questions in the individual chapters.

- How long has the person been in their role, and what's their career trajectory?
- What are their aspirations for the future?
- What is the structure of their department, and why did they choose it?
- What is the composition of their senior team? Their strengths and areas for development? Their length of service?
- Who are their high-potential individuals, and how are they managing them?
- What is going well and what is frustrating them?
- And the most important question of them all: "How can I help you?" It's simple and disarming, and it often produces some of the most open and insightful responses. Practice that servant leadership with your people, and you'll both succeed.

5. INFORMATION TECHNOLOGY

What this department does

Your IT department partners with all parts of the organisation to understand and to deliver its technology needs. From implementing strategic solutions to meeting the day-to-day needs of staff, IT may play anything from a key support role to occupying the centre-stage of the organisation. Either way, it's fundamental to your perceived success and to the success of the organisation.

IT is a tough area. It's often the first place where the need for change is first felt, and it's expected to be the first to react. IT professionals live in a world where the drivers of change are stronger and faster, and the expectations continually rise. They have to balance old and new technologies, control the total cost of ownership and explain their value to sceptical senior management. The COO is a critical ally and a champion of IT.

Roles and responsibilities

- **Strategy and architecture.** With the goals of the organisation in mind, the IT department decides on the vision for the core architecture of IT, the standard platforms it will use and how decisions will be made about building software in house vs. buying it – the organisation's "philosophy" regarding technology. Often overlooked or considered theoretical, this is the skeleton of IT and the solid foundation upon which future (expensive and significant) decisions about technology will be made.

- **Business analysis.** Taking the problems and the needs of the organisation and structuring them into a properly defined set of requirements or *functional* specifications, from which *technical* specifications can be written. This includes business process mapping and re-engineering to optimise processes prior to automating them.
- **Software design and development.** Using the outputs from business analysis and either writing the code or configuring services for new or enhanced applications. The way software is developed can be approached in a number of ways from the traditional waterfall to the agile method. There is a growing tendency towards integrating development and operations into DevOps teams.
- **System testing.** Once new code is designed, this area manages the process of testing it before it's used in the live environment. There are three levels of testing:
  1. **System testing** – performed by IT staff. Ensures the system operates according to technical specifications.
  2. **User testing** – performed by business users. Ensures the system operates according to functional specifications. This also includes assessing the user experience.
  3. **Regression testing** – performance of a specific set of core functionality tests on a repetitive basis. Sometimes automated, this ensures new additions to code don't break existing functionality.

- **Security and maintenance of the production environment**. Controlling the promotion of new code or services to the production and wider environment, ensuring no unauthorised or untested upgrades jeopardise the smooth running of the live systems.
- **Application support**. Managing scheduled maintenance and upgrades, which may require system outages and downtime.
- **Vendor agreements / software licencing**. Working with the Supply Chain team to agree on the optimal licencing structure for purchased software (e.g., individual user licences or single enterprise-wide licence, fixed vs. variable pricing, individual vs. bulk packages, etc.).
- **Database management**. Dedicated database management systems, such as Oracle or SQL, sit underneath the technologies that staff use every day. Database managers design and maintain the data warehouses that underpin user applications.
- **User / desktop support**. Handling user queries and calls, dealing with forgotten passwords, laptop requests, new application requests, etc.
- **Service management**. A set of activities based on policies and structured processes to plan, design, deliver and operate IT services offered to customers. This is typically approached using frameworks such as ITIL (Information Technology Infrastructure Library) and/or COBIT (Control Objectives for Information and Related Technologies).
- **Information Security (InfoSec)**. Designing and implementing a framework of controls to protect the IT

environment. InfoSec may be part of the IT or Risk department. It's responsible for setting an overall vision and strategy, assigning roles and responsibilities, establishing firewall and perimeter security, checking access to systems, training users and raising awareness.

- **Knowledge management / learning.** Capturing knowledge about IT systems, code, application programming interfaces, and database protocols and documenting it in a place and a manner that can be easily retrieved by future developers. This is like the instruction manual for the entire IT system. Lose this, and future generations of IT developers will have to resort to reading thousands of lines of code to figure out what their predecessors were doing. Because IT people typically know how to catalogue information well, they're sometimes charged with knowledge management for the organisation on a broader basis.

- **Talent management.** Talented IT staff are perennially in high demand. Your CIO/Head of IT should have career progression and talent development plans in place to attract, retain and motivate your brightest and most sought-after assets. Beyond standard learning and development, IT staff want to work in an environment where they can learn and push the boundaries to maximise their value to the organisation.

- **Business continuity / disaster recovery.** Working in conjunction with the risk team, developing Business Impact Analyses, system failover plans, system backup routines and hot site facilities – so that if your server room fails, you can recover and restore operations (see Risk chapter for further information).

Enterprise Architecture

At the core of your IT function should be a strong sense of the desired technology architecture, linked to the achievement of organisational goals. Too often these are theoretical documents rather than a solid backbone on which to base technology decisions.

As COO, you should observe the relationship between system users and technology when making IT decisions. Who owns the technology budgets? Who takes ownership of the software? What's the process by which user needs are defined? Who defines the problems that need to be solved? How are initiatives prioritised across the enterprise? Watch for conflicts where siloes exist within the organisation. Who wins – those who shout loudest or those who add true value?

There's also the risk that technology architecture becomes overly theoretical and not grounded in reality. Your technologists must be solution-focused and must answer the question, "What problem are we trying to solve?"

Examine where Enterprise Architecture sits in the organisation and who it answers to. When a casting vote is needed between the architects and the users, who provides it? It might well be you.

Overlaps

Increasingly, non-technology users are becoming more technical in nature and responsibilities between IT and other departments are blurring. For example, in Investment Banking, traders are highly adept at creating their own financial models, some with quite sophisticated embedded coding. In Marketing, many roles are becoming increasingly digital in nature, with roles in user experience and content management sitting somewhere in between the two departments.

Business continuity and disaster recovery should be managed jointly with the Risk and the Operations teams.

InfoSec can be viewed either as a technical function or as a second-line risk function, but I believe it sits more naturally as part of Risk.

Relationships to watch

Technology and Supply Chain need to work together collaboratively, as some of the most strategic and expensive investments take place in technology. You may find that the Technology team will want to progress with a preferred vendor, while the Supply Chain team will want to tender to multiple vendors, avoiding cosy relationships and kickbacks. Ensure your Supply Chain team is given the background and the context to IT – it pays off when IT can explain what they're trying to achieve and why.

Industry frameworks

There is a wealth of frameworks out there for different aspects of IT, but only a few which cover the breadth of what IT management is about:

1. COBIT (Control OBjectives for Information and related Technologies) is an internationally recognised framework for IT management and governance.
2. ITIL (Information Technology Infrastructure Library) is a framework for service management in IT. Linked to that is ISO/IEC 20000 (the first international standard for IT service management).
3. ISO 27001 is the most recognised industry standard for InfoSec.

The major aspects of these frameworks are summarised below.

COBIT

COBIT 5 was released in 2012. It is built around five core principles:

1. Meeting stakeholder needs, or in other words, aligning the IT strategy with the business strategy
2. Covering the enterprise end-to-end
3. Applying a single integrated framework
4. Enabling a holistic approach
5. Separating governance from management

Useful COBIT components include:

- A framework which organises IT governance objectives and good practices by four IT "domains" and links them to business requirements
- Process descriptions for every part of the organisation
- Control objectives for each IT process
- Management guidelines on assignment of responsibilities, objectives and performance measurement
- Maturity models which assess the maturity of each process

ITIL

ITIL is a globally recognised best-practice framework to support how IT is delivered. It aims to ensure that IT supports the overall goals of the organisation and that it delivers IT services optimally. It's aligned to ISO 20000.

The ITIL framework contains the following elements:

IT service management	1. Service Support
	2. Service Delivery
Operational guidance	3. ICT infrastructure management
	4. Security management
	5. Application management
	6. Software asset management
Implementation	7. Planning to implement service management
Guidelines for smaller IT units	8. ITIL small-scale implementation

ITIL provides a range of capabilities for IT, allowing it to:

- Support business outcomes
- Enable business change
- Manage risk in line with business needs
- Optimise the customer experience
- Demonstrate value for money
- Ensure continuous improvement

The purported benefits of implementing ITIL range from minimising service disruption, to positive business relationships, to higher quality, to better ROI.

ISO 27001

ISO 27001 is the international framework for Information Security Management. It encompasses all of the controls – legal, physical and technical – that should be part of an organisation's information risk management processes. ISO 27001 is technology-neutral, that is, it should be capable of implementation regardless of the technology in place, and it requires buy-in from the whole organisation. It defines a six-part planning process:

1. Define security policy
2. Define the scope of the Information Security Management System
3. Assess risk
4. Manage identified risks
5. Select the controls to be implemented
6. Prepare the statement of applicability

The specification includes roles and responsibilities, documentation standards, internal audits, continual improvement, and corrective and preventive action.

Supporting ISO 27001 is ISO 27002 – a set of information security control objectives and generally accepted good practices. ISO 27002 contains 12 main sections:

1. Risk assessment
2. Security policy
3. Organisation of information security
4. Asset management
5. Human resources security
6. Physical and environmental security
7. Communications and operations management
8. Access control
9. Information systems acquisition, development and maintenance
10. Information security incident management
11. Business continuity management
12. Compliance

Organisations can seek to become ISO 27001 accredited. If your organisation has not gone the whole way in achieving ISO accreditation, this isn't necessarily a problem. However, I would expect to see evidence that the organisation has benchmarked itself against the standards, is aware of its shortcomings and is working to remediate areas where it falls short.

ISO 27005 is an Information Security Risk Management standard. Other related standards under development in the 27000 category are:

27003 – Guidance on how to implement the framework

27004 – Measurement standards including metrics to help improve the effectiveness of Information Security Management

27006 - A guide to certification

27007 – Information Security auditing guidelines

Being prepared for cyber-attacks

Cyber-attacks are frequently cited as one of the top risks facing organisations today. Expect it to gain more traction following the recent global cyber-ransom attack. As COO, you should be working with your CIO/Head of Technology to:

1. Ensure the cyber risk to the organisation is understood – which business lines, functions and departments will be impacted and how. Include particularly the revenue-generating arm of the organisation, media, websites, etc.
2. Ensure cyber security risk is on the organisation's risk register, assessed and mitigated. This risk is moving constantly so it requires regular review.
3. Resource your IT team appropriately to deal with the challenges - and listen to their concerns.
4. Educate employees on the risks.
5. Leverage external networks for support and best practice.

6. Ensure cyber-attacks are an integral part of your organisation's business continuity and disaster recovery plans.

Warning signs

The following are indications of potential problems in Technology:

Obsolete technology and / or lack of a maintenance / upgrade plan. Signs of a lack of investment, lack of ambition, or both.

Frequent outages. Often a symptom of poor maintenance or weak testing and implementation.

Staff disaffection with technology – or a lack of awareness of what staff think of technology. If your Head of Technology doesn't know how the user experience is perceived, why not commission a staff survey to find out what they like and don't like?

Public disaffection with your technology / high abandonment rate. If you sell online, are you having a lot of customers turn away at some point in the purchase process?

At Save the Children, we noticed that it required six different pages / clicks to donate to us. We worked on removing as many of those steps as possible and on making it very user friendly to donate. The result? Increased conversion of interest to donations.

Good to great

So, you have established that your IT department has a good vision and architecture, linked to the strategy of the organisation. It is well run, in accordance with industry standards. How can you take it to the next level?

From support service to value delivery. Progressive IT departments should be looking at all aspects of the organisation and how they can be improved by technology. Can technology improve or even bypass current processes? What is the cost of doing things as they are today? Can technology find a different way?

Innovation. Because of the scrum and/or rapid application development processes that have been around in IT for over 20 years now, IT staff are more able to adapt and innovate than others. They're accustomed to coming up with beta versions of products quickly, testing, failing fast and learning. Could those concepts be applied more widely in your organisation? You could leverage your IT staff to find out.

Strong relationships inside and out. Ideally, you want your CIO to have a healthy dialogue with all parts of the organisation without you needing to intervene. How close is your CIO to the revenue-generating parts of the organisation? Could you bring them closer? Equally, it's in your interest for your CIO to be well-networked outside the organisation.

Setting the strategic agenda for digital. You'd have to live under a rock to not realise the impact digital strategies are having on organisations, products, services, markets and consumers. In a very short space of time, whole new industries are opening up. Challenger organisations, with low barriers to entry, are threatening industry giants. You, your CIO and technology team need to be attuned to this, constantly learning and adapting to new disruptors. Staying agile and at the same time staying the course on the major pieces of work is one of the most challenging balances for organisations to achieve.

Current hot topics

Blockchain. Blockchain is a distributed ledger technology that originally underpinned the bitcoin cryptocurrency. Increasingly, financial and other sectors are seeing the potential of this technology to solve many information security challenges, such as identity verification, authentication and non-repudiation of contracts.

Software as a service / "the cloud." Rather than big bulky servers being installed in IT rooms, IT teams now want Software as a Service ("SaaS"), where software exists in the cloud and is leased rather than owned. Most contracts with big application providers now span three years, with review periods built in. This provides more flexibility, less maintenance and less need for physical hardware. Of course, it comes at a cost, but this is the direction the industry is moving in.

Cyber security. One of the top risks for organisations in the current environment. Recent events may mean there is more appetite at Board and Executive level to spend on mitigating cyber risk than before.

Evolving roles – e.g., marketing / digital. As already stated, digital is increasingly permeating all our roles, starting with the tasks that are easier to automate but increasingly moving up the value chain, even into areas such as accountancy and law. Staff in all sectors will need to become more digitally savvy to know how to utilise and to harness these technologies and inject their personal judgement / empathy appropriately. This has implications for jobs, job descriptions, organisational structure and target operating model design.

Internet of things (IoT). The rise of connected devices from consumer goods to sophisticated industrial tools is changing the landscape for data and cyber security. Whether your trade is kettles, toasters, ATMs, life support machines or submarines, your organisation is likely to be impacted. You need to be ready to embrace both the opportunities and the threats that may arise.

Scrum / agile technologies. In the olden days we all followed lovely waterfall techniques to deliver software. Business analysts, together with users, defined their requirements in increasing levels of detail, then developers built them from the ground up.

Now, most modern IT professionals and business users find that approach slow and inflexible, and are keen to embrace more agile methodologies. "Scrum" and "agile" are terms used interchangeably to mean rapid code development and getting a minimum viable product quickly to the end user for them to test and give feedback on. It's typically high energy, with short timelines.

Advantages and disadvantages of scrum:

Advantages	Disadvantages
✓ Quick	✗ Can involve significant rework
✓ Early sight of new product	✗ Less applicable to older ERP (Enterprise Resource Planning) systems
✓ Users like the energy	

Two-speed technology. If you're in a mid-size to large organisation, chances are you will have one, or several, Enterprise Resource Planning systems – the big finance and value chain systems such as SAP and Oracle – that serve as the backbone to many organisations. Organisations can't live with these systems and can't live without them. One very large retailer told me that it would cost them tens of millions of pounds to take theirs out. Few have the money or the desire for this. So the dilemma is how to offer a great digital experience to front-end users and customers, with twenty-plus-year-old monolithic systems in the background. Some believe the answer is twin-speed technology. Gartner calls this the bi-modal concept, and it has attracted some controversy.

Bimodal IT means doing sufficient maintenance on your ERP system to keep it stable, and developing cutting-edge rapid solutions which interact with your old technology via interfaces. Done well it allows established organisations such as John Lewis in the UK and Ford Motors in the US to create excellent digital capability and to compete with newer entrants to the market. The dangers of this are well documented – all those interfaces into the ERP system are complex and fragile, requiring testing and maintenance. Secondly, there is the risk of creating a two-step technology team with all the young, hip rising stars working on digital and others being confined to the "legacy" systems. This can lead to problems with culture and morale.

BYOD (bring your own device). Hardly "hot" any more but still being adopted relatively slowly by organisations. Good value for money and seamless for the employee, as long as you can get the security right.

Agile working. The nature of work is changing. How, when and where people work is becoming more agile, more self-managed. Technology is supporting this through the use of always available, location-agnostic services such as Windows 365 and laptops with dual operating systems for work and personal use.

Ten questions to ask your CIO / Head of IT

1. What is the Enterprise Architecture and the strategy of IT? How is it adding value to the organisation?
2. What are the current strengths and weaknesses of the technology offering today?
3. What are the key applications used by the organisation in Finance, Operations, Customer Relationship Management, HR? How well understood/documented are they?
4. How easy is it to make changes to the environment? How often are changes made? What is the proportion between the successful changes vs. the rolled-back changes?

5. What are the key vendor relationships? Who manages master software agreements and licensing?
6. What approach is taken to Service Management? What are the end user perceptions of the IT service?
7. Where are IT teams located and how do they service the organisation (e.g., is there a "follow the sun" service desk that services users on a 24-hour basis from sites across the world)?
8. How are major systems backed up? How frequently? When were they last tested?
9. When was IT last audited? What were the findings?
10. How is the IT department approaching innovation?

Checklist of policies

- Technology strategy / Enterprise architecture document – what systems, platforms, databases and applications the organisation will acquire
- Procurement – how people go about requesting and sourcing hardware (laptops, desktops)
- IT service manual / catalogue – the list of services the IT function performs and, ideally, the service levels it sets
- E-mail / internet use policy
- Information Security Policy

Further reading

http://www.ey.com/gl/en/services/advisory/ey-cio-program

www.isaca.org/cobit

https://www.axelos.com/Corporate/media/Files/Misc%20Qualific
ation%20Docs/ITIL_Value_Proposition-(1).pdf

https://www.agilebusiness.org/

http://www.scaledagileframework.com/

http://www.kanomodel.com/

6. FINANCE

What this department does

The Finance department is charged with guarding the money – from daily cash management to the strategic sourcing and allocation of capital, from setting budgets to monitoring performance, from identifying variances to maintaining the financial control environment to publishing the statutory annual accounts of the organisation. The CFO and the COO typically operate very closely together – sometimes as peers, sometimes with the CFO reporting to the COO.

The Finance team is likely to be one of the largest support services teams in the organisation, and one of the most visible. Many COOs come to the role as former chartered or management accountants. The ability to read the numbers is an important skill to the COO. However, you don't need to have years of accounting experience. It's more important that you see the trends and the issues – the story behind the numbers.

Spend time getting to know your CFO. Understand their strengths and their weaknesses, and see how you can achieve synergy. A good relationship with your CFO will provide you with depth, strength and perspective on how the finances can deliver the strategy. Differing styles can work well – I once worked with quite an optimistic, upbeat CFO who was a good foil to my tendency to focus on the risks. Too similar and you can trip over and frustrate each other.

> **Case study: Looking ahead**
>
> A good CFO always looks forward – to the next quarter, year, five years – to see what macro trends are happening and how they'll affect the organisation's financial model. When your CFO is concerned, listen. I remember how a relatively new CFO of the organisation I worked in at the time published a set of projections that showed we could be in financial difficulty the following year, if a set of scenarios played out. We implemented a stage-gate process where discretionary funding was held back pending the outcome of certain events. Fortunately, events turned out better than they might have, and we were able to open the funding gates again. We then put in place a long-range planning model showing the outcome of different variables on our working capital and reserves, so that we couldn't be surprised again. It was an early warning for me on the importance of listening to finance and looking ahead.

Roles and responsibilities

The CFO is concerned primarily with four key questions:

1. Do we have enough cash / bank facilities? In other words, liquidity.
2. Do we know where we make money? For decision support.
3. Are there sufficient controls to protect the assets in the business? The Financial Control environment
4. Are we making the right investments? Investment appraisal.

Liquidity

The CFO is charged with ensuring the organisation has access to enough cash and bank facilities to service its operations. The CFO will set the liquidity policy, specifying the length of time (usually 12-24 months) the organisation could continue its operations in the event the capital markets become inaccessible. Liquidity and cash flow are the lifeblood of the organisation. Even a profitable organisation can run out of liquidity. In fact, growing businesses are particularly susceptible. A good CFO will always be on top of liquidity.

Activities in this area include:

- **Financial control / finance operations**
    - o **Cash management.** Monitoring money coming in and out. Petty cash. Expenses management. Day to day balancing of short-term deposits and credit. Bank reconciliations.
    - o **Accounts payable.** Approving invoices to be paid. Setting payment terms and chasing payments from customers.
    - o **Accounts receivable / credit control.** Setting credit terms and monitoring payments from customers.
    - o **Production / cost accounting.** Overseeing and calculating production / manufacturing costs.
    - o **Taxation.** Tax planning, calculation and settlement, dealing with the relevant authorities in each jurisdiction. Filing of timely and accurate tax returns.

- o **Payroll**. Managing all aspects of getting employees paid: on-boarding, correct tax calculations, pension deductions, benefits, termination.
- o **Insurance**. This may be part of the finance or the Risk team. Identifying the types of insurance required by the organisation, liaising with brokers, evaluating tenders, selecting policies and maintaining insurance renewals.

- **Treasury / capital management**. Looking strategically at the capital structure of the organisation and monitoring its medium to long-term requirements. Examining the capital structure (reserves, loans, cash, investments, deposits) and coming up with the optimal structure to meet the needs of the organisation.
- **Purchasing / vendor management / supply chain.** This may or may not be part of Finance. The finance department is likely to have a role to play in approving invoices for payment, subject to the limits set for the organisation.

Decision support

The CFO should know where the organisation makes money: by market, product and customer segment. The CFO should be a commercial voice at the table looking back at actual performance and making sure future commercial deals, forecasts and business plans all hit the right level of profitability. This is why an outgoing, visible, commercially-focused CFO is so valuable – customer contact and understanding of profitability, past and future, are important.

- o **Budgeting / income and expenditure projection**. Setting budgets on departmental or project level for the whole organisation for the year ahead. Working with individual departments on their best, worst and most likely case scenarios. Understanding the drivers that will affect the eventual outcome and the risks and the opportunities that may influence them. Planning sufficient contingency to meet the most likely range of outcomes.
- o **Forecasting**. In-year review of performance. Monitoring changes to the environment and adjusting the forecast for the year-end accordingly.
- o **Management reporting**. Publication (usually monthly) of a set of results used by Management. These may include operational as well as financial numbers, e.g., volumes and other key performance indicators.

Control environment

The CFO should set the tone and the standard for the control environment as it relates to Finance. You, the CFO and the CRO (Chief Risk Officer), form the first line of defence against risks (I explain this in the Risk chapter). Activities that fall within this remit are:

- • **Risk Management**
  - o **Financial risk management.** Understanding credit, market and operational risks and using financial instruments to hedge the exposure, e.g., the use of

commodity instruments by an airline to hedge fuel costs.

- o **Product control.** This term can mean different things in different sectors. In investment banking, product control is a specialist function that oversees the trading activities of the front office, ensuring they stay within the set limits.
- o **Maintenance of financial control environment.** This includes responsibility for the design and the operation of all processes that maintain the integrity of the financial system: key finance systems, creation and maintenance of the chart of accounts, definition of roles and responsibilities, segregation of duties, error management, etc. It ensures appropriate controls and limits around *who* in the organisation can spend *how much* and on *what*.

- **Management of relationship with external auditor.** Working throughout the year with the organisation's chosen financial auditor. This is likely to include at least one site visit a year for control assessment purposes, in addition to the year-end procedures.
- **Reporting**
    - o **Project reporting.** Reporting on the project's cost, progress and financial benefits – did it achieve its income / cost reduction objectives?
    - o **Statutory reporting / annual reporting.** Publication of the official, audited accounts of the organisation and filing with the appropriate regulator: Companies Office, Charities Commission, etc. This includes fulfilling

capital adequacy requirements and verifying that the company can remain a going concern in the following year.

- **Intercompany reconciliation.** If you have a federated organisation made up of different entities/companies in different countries, this involves managing the complex set of reconciliations between them. It also includes the thorny issue of transfer pricing, which has significant taxation implications.

Investment appraisal

The CFO appraises the organisation's investments in working capital (new customers, inventory, credit terms, etc.), capital expenditure (new plant, IT, etc.) and Mergers & Acquisitions. The CFO is accountable to the Board and to the organisation's investors for appraising the investment decisions the organisation wishes to make.

- **Asset Management**
  - **Fixed asset management.** Maintenance of the fixed asset register, from buildings to machines, from cars to computers. Decisions about valuation and depreciation. Tracking, controlling and accounting for maintenance costs. Reporting on loss, waste, obsolescence and fraud.
  - **Investment management.** Management of the organisation's investment portfolio and financial assets according to the set objective, strategy and investment plan.

- **Investor relations.** If your organisation is publicly quoted, it will have to report to its shareholders and deal with quarterly analyst calls and reporting. The CFO plays a central role in the Initial Public Offering when taking a company public.
- **Mergers and acquisitions.** Assessing potential targets in the market for merger / acquisition and handling due diligence and valuation activities to assure the Executive team and the Board they're getting the best acquisition for the price.
- **Actuarial / pension management.** Management of the organisation's pension obligations (including obligations under defined benefit schemes), investment decisions and pension fund deficit. This specialist activity is often overseen by a dedicated independent pensions committee.

Overlaps

The CFO and the COO relationship is crucial. Like you, the CFO works with all parts of the organisation, including:

- Sales on forecasting and budgets, as well as credit control and receivables;
- Operations for cost control and production reporting;
- HR on headcount and payroll;
- Technology in areas of major capital spending, plus depreciation;
- Risk, Legal and other support areas in designing appropriately controlled systems and processes.

Relationships to watch

The interaction between Sales and the Finance department can be strained. There's always a temptation for the front office to inflate targets and overstate performance, relying on the CFO to match it to reality. Equally, a very upbeat CEO who sees only the upside can be challenging for the CFO who has to bring everyone's expectations back to reality.

Industry frameworks

In the English-speaking world the main frameworks underpinning Finance are the UK and the US Generally Accepted Accounting Principles ("GAAP") – accounting treatments and conventions for how organisations report their financial performance. In the UK the FRC (Financial Reporting Council) is responsible for regulatory oversight.

International Financial Reporting Standards ("IFRS") are a set of accounting standards maintained by the International Accounting Standards Board. These standards are used in more than 100 countries, including the EU (European Union) and most of the G20 countries.

Banking organisations must also comply with the Basel II systems for internal controls and capital adequacy requirements.

Publicly quoted companies must comply with SOX (Sarbanes-Oxley) regulations.

Sarbanes-Oxley ("SOX" or "Sarbox" in brief)

The Sarbanes-Oxley Act of 2002 (written by two accountants who self-named the regulation) was passed in the US in 2002 in response to several accounting scandals, including those of Enron and Worldcom. The main two provisions of SOX are Sections 302 and 404.

Section 302 requires senior management to certify the accuracy of their reported financial statements.

Section 404 requires management and auditors to establish and maintain internal controls supporting the financial statements, and to report on the adequacy of those controls.

SOX also contains provisions relating to the maintenance of electronic records, destruction and falsification of records, the retention period for storing records and the specific types of business records that need to be maintained.

SOX has not been universally popular. Critics argue it has added a lot of red tape and expense and little in the way of real controls. Whether or not it remains as is under the new US administration remains to be seen.

Taxation. In the UK, HMRC (Her Majesty's Revenue and Customs) designs and oversees tax. In the US, the main body is the IRS (Internal Revenue Service) with taxes levied at federal, state and local government levels.

In the UK pensions are regulated by the Pensions Regulator. In the US the main law governing the 401(k) pension plans is the ERISA (Employee Retirement Income Security Act)

If the company is publicly quoted, there will be listing and reporting rules from the relevant exchanges (FTSE, NYSE, NASDAQ, etc.).

Monthly reporting

A key element of governance and decision support in any organisation is the monthly report produced by the Finance department. The monthly finance reporting pack should contain the following at a minimum:

- Overall headlines / executive summary.
- Financial summary; income and expenditure by major department line. This may include comparison to last month, to forecast or to last year's same period.
- Top line analysis of the drivers behind that month's performance.
- Income further analysis – divisional, by drivers, by product area, etc.
- Expenditure further analysis – as above.
- Cash/debt/reserves. Movement month to month and reasons why. Variance from expectations / thresholds.
- Projections to end of year – constantly updated and based on rolling information.
- Risks and opportunities for discussion – what might cause upside or downside variance to expectations for management to consider and take action on.
- Further divisional analysis as needed in the appendices.

Warning signs

Warning lights should come on if you see any of the below:

- **Fluctuating cash balances / balances below thresholds.** These may be signs that variability of income is not being actively managed or that the organisation is struggling.
- **Lack of thresholds / targets for key financial ratios.** Could indicate an immature system of financial control.
- **Month-end accounts** that take a long time (e.g., three weeks plus) to be published. This could be an indication of sub-optimal procedures or systems. It means that the organisation is flying blind for much of the time, taking almost a whole extra month to hear about and respond to changes in forecasts.
- **Lack of control over fixed assets / mobile assets.** Could indicate that controls over acquisition, tracking, return and disposal need to be strengthened.
- **Negative working capital / payments to suppliers and from customers being protracted.** Could indicate weaknesses in the procurement system, issues with the products/services the organisation is supplying or insufficient working capital management.
- **Substantial variances to budget and forecast.** Something is not turning out the way the organisation expected or the organisation doesn't have reliable forecasting.
- **A CEO who disregards Finance or has a difficult relationship with the department.** This may lead to a disenfranchised CFO and de-motivated Finance team. It may also mean that warnings are not picked up early enough. As COO, you'll need to add your political weight

and explain the financials to the CEO in a way that they will listen.

- **Dwindling reserves.** An indication of gradual decline in the organisation and / or lack of proactive action by management (see Kids Company case study in Governance chapter).

- **A product portfolio that is not diversified.** Where are the growth products or services? Which ones are the cash cows? Is there a conversation taking place at executive level about the new products / the balance of investment between existing and new offerings?

Good to great

A great Finance department and CFO are integral partners to all parts of the organisation. They understand the strategy and the numbers, headcount, projections and forecasts. Below are the ways in which they can further optimise their contribution:

Digital. The more processes can be automated, the tighter they'll become and the less administrative finance personnel you'll need to manage them.

Strengthening ethics and governance. A strong CFO should play a central role in defining the governance framework of the organisation and in setting the tone for ethics and good practice. You may well be each other's wingmen when reporting to the Board and in other settings.

Financial optimisation. A strong CFO will seek out ways to reduce expenses – payroll costs, waste in the value chain, losses due to fraud – as well as contribute ideas to boost sales and optimise operational costs.

Current hot topics

It's calming down now, but the **implementation of FRS 102** (the Financial Reporting Standard applicable in the UK and Republic of Ireland) had significant implications for revenue recognition, in many cases requiring previous years' income to be re-stated.

Procure to pay software is being actively considered and implemented by Finance departments for its role in automating and tightening procurement (tendering, ordering, receiving, matching, paying for inbound goods and services).

Offshoring of functions, e.g., product control. As offshoring matures, increasingly complex activities such as product control and accounting are starting to come into scope, with higher level financial advisory activities remaining closer to home - for the time being.

Pension funds. The management of deficits, moving staff to defined contribution schemes and where and how to invest the pension fund are all likely hot topics for the CFO, Executive and Board. There are plenty of public examples of how *not* to do this, with the organisations concerned suffering significant reputational damage.

Checklist of policies

- Delegation of Authority and authorisation of payments / limits

- Investment management policy
- Expenses policy
- Reserves policy
- Taxation policy

Ten questions to ask Finance

1. What are the key sources and categories of income and expenditure?
2. How is the organisation benchmarking vs. others in the same sector on financial indicators?
3. According to the CFO, what are the most telling financial statistics about the organisation?
4. Are there defined pension benefit obligations? Is the pension fund in surplus or deficit?
5. What are the key variables influencing the finances of the organisation (e.g., foreign exchange rates, interest rates, commodity prices)?
6. Staff costs and trends. What is the headcount? What proportion of overall costs does payroll represent? What is the blend of fixed and variable staffing?
7. What are the main finance systems? How well do they interface? Where are the integration issues / points of weakness?
8. How long after year-end are the statutory accounts published?
9. What are the key year-end valuations that require judgement?
10. What concerns were raised in the past year by the auditors?

Further reading

Drysdale, A.: "The Financial Controller"

7. Human Resources

What this department does

Human Resources (HR) assesses the needs of the organisation (linked to the strategy) and helps acquire, develop and position the best talent available, at a certain price point, to achieve organisational goals and beat the competition. The Director of HR reports to the COO or to the CEO.

> Good HR management will help foster a strong culture, a motivated work force, high performance, deep organisational memory and know-how – all at the right cost to the organisation. Weak HR management will manifest as a weak or toxic culture, inability to source or to retain talent, loss of key resources, operational friction and over-paying for short-term contractors.

When the people management side of the organisation isn't working, everything is hard. Executive Management and the Board will wonder why performance is suffering, why projects don't get completed on time and why the organisation keeps making the same mistakes time and again.

Some CEOs instinctively understand people management – they feel comfortable in the company of people and express genuine interest in their lives. Others appear folksy and friendly on the outside, but on the inside act in a Machiavellian manner. Still others don't understand the value proposition of good, strategic

HR Management and treat it either with disdain, discomfort or neglect.

As COO, your engagement with HR will need to reflect, and sometimes compensate for, the CEO's style. If your CEO has low EQ, is numbers-focused and autocratic, you'll need to intervene to translate the CEO's strategy to the entire organisation, inspiring people to get behind it. If your CEO has high EQ, you can play the role of reinforcing partner, and focus your energies elsewhere. Either way, a strong partnership between the COO and the HR Director will be mutually beneficial, reinforcing you both and making you stronger than the sum of your parts.

HR staff have a very distinct set of skills. They absorb people's issues every day. Typically right-sided thinkers, they need strong interpersonal skills, boundless resilience in dealing with people, and enthusiasm for talent development, knowledge and learning. On top of it they must possess in-depth knowledge of employee relations law and operate with forensic precision when completing processes such as redundancy rounds or annual pay reviews. HR doesn't have to be bureaucratic or even "nice," but it must be effective. Take a look at Netflix's HR policy for a powerful example of a policy that's not particularly "nice" yet is clear and empowering.

Some HR departments hide behind processes to avoid saying yes to new ideas. They operate merely as people processing departments, high on procedures and administration and low on value delivery. The CEO who has experienced only this kind of HR is usually sceptical about the HR department's contribution. In this case you need to show your CEO the possibilities of HR, that the organisation *is* the people and that without them nothing else matters. A commercially-focused HR department, one that truly understands the organisation and aligns the management of people behind it, is a valuable asset and is worth holding on to.

Your HR Director may need to play a delicate role in moderating the relationships at the top of the organisation. This can be awkward and exhausting – the HR Director has very few people they can go to for advice. If you can foster a relationship with your HRD where they feel it's safe to confide in you, they'll be enormously grateful – and you'll be rewarded with a better understanding of what makes your organisation tick.

On the flip-side, if you get the tone, the messaging or the execution of key people management processes wrong, the organisation will face a world of pain. Resignations, industrial action, tribunals and negative PR are just some of the delights your organisation will have to deal with. Don't be one of those organisations.

Roles and responsibilities

- **Strategic resource and talent planning**. HR management starts with the organisation's strategy. The HR function that isn't starting with strategy can be only operational at best.

- **Recruitment.** Defining the recruitment strategy to create a healthy pipeline of talent. This includes supporting the organisation with position management, advertising, screening, interviewing, selecting and on-boarding new staff.
- **On-boarding and induction**. Overseeing a new recruit's all-important first contact with the organisation and speeding the transition of new staff from net cost items to value contributors.
- **Performance management.** Setting a framework, policy and processes for assessment of staff performance. Supporting management through these processes and linking to promotion, development and remuneration.
- **Staff development / talent management.** Taking into account the needs of the organisation, creating a framework for how staff will learn and develop, both on the job and in formal training sessions. Starting with mandatory, compliance-driven training through to high-powered, one-on-one executive coaching. Includes the

identification of high potential individuals and the management of their journey through the organisation.

- **Reward.** Setting the reward framework for the organisation, working with the Board of Directors or a separate Remuneration Committee. This includes everything from executive pay to overall payroll ranges, linked to role descriptions. Embraces fixed and variable compensation, and employee benefits.
- **Management of employee benefits.** Health insurance, gym membership, season ticket loans – design and management of the suite of benefits that will attract and retain the people the organisation wants.
- **Terminations, resignations, redundancy.** Supporting the different ways in which staff can exit an organisation, from being walked off the premises to a happy retirement.
- **Employee relations / legal.** Advising management in understanding, interpreting and applying employment law and regulation fairly, equitably and consistently in all dealings with staff.
  - o Whistleblowing. A particular aspect of employee relations that provides specific legal protections for a person who "blows the whistle" on wrongdoing, as long as they do it in good faith. This area may be overseen by the Risk or Compliance department.
  - o Grievances. Managing the process where an employee is dissatisfied with some aspect of their treatment and has made a complaint.

- o Disciplinary and capability processes. Supporting management in dealing with issues of underperformance of staff members.
- **Business partnering.** Many HR functions assign generalist business partners to particular entities or divisions. These partners act as overall points of contact to support parts of the organisation. They will liaise with specialist HR teams as required, for complex issues.
- **Staff engagement.** Working with the Executive team and with Internal Communications, assessing the level of staff engagement in the organisation and creating plans to improve it.

Overlaps

As with the CFO, HR typically pervades the organisation. Particular areas of overlap include:

- With Legal – on Employee Relations issues.
- With Executive and Middle Management – on organisational design, succession planning, recruitment, performance and remuneration.
- With Facilities – on employee health & safety issues.
- With Finance – on remuneration and payroll.

Relationships to watch

How much does the CEO embrace the HRD's people agenda? Do the hiring managers follow the recruitment processes as designed or are they just trying to get people in the door as quickly as possible? Do line managers properly assume their people management responsibilities or do they expect HR to manage people for them?

A pervading attitude amongst some managers is that their job is to deliver the numbers, not to manage people. At times, managers shirk their HR responsibilities, either because of lack of courage to hold tough conversations, lack of interest or lack of time. It's not HR's job to manage people, but it is HR's job to support managers in doing so.

Industry frameworks

The Dave Ulrich competency model for HR[20] is one of the most recognised - and debated - HR frameworks. In its latest iteration, it categorises HR competencies into nine categories:

1. Strategic positioner – interpreting the business context, decoding stakeholder expectations and understanding internal business operations
2. Credible activist – influencing and relating to others, earning trust through results
3. Capability builder
4. Change champion – designing culture and managing change
5. HR Innovator and Integrator

In the UK, the Chartered Institute of Professional Development ("CIPD") offers consultancy, support and training in the areas of:

- Employment law

---

[20] Ulrich, D.: "HR from the outside in: Six competencies for the future of Human Resources", 2012

- Employment relationship (including diversity, employee engagement, flexible working and absence management)
- Attracting, developing and retaining the right people (including recruitment, induction, pay and benefits, performance management and people development)

There is also a substantial body of labour legislation and case history in which your Employee Relations team should be fluent.

Organisational design

One of the most important joint responsibilities for you and your HR Director is organisational design. Chances are that as part of your, and your CEO's, tenure, you'll seek to re-design some or all of the organisation. Take your direction from the organisation's strategy, culture and desired target operating model. Your Director of HR will play a pivotal role in this process.

We all know the stories about organisational design that hasn't gone well – one boss wants the organisation vertically aligned (to provide better end-to-end visibility of processes and agility), the next wants it horizontally aligned (for better efficiency and control), and so line managers get switched around back and forth, staff shrug their shoulders and try to get on with the job.

How do you avoid these pitfalls? I like the "10 Principles of Organization Design" described by Gary L. Neilson, Jaime

Estupiñán and Bhushan Sethi[21], which, among other recommendations, says that you should

1. Declare **amnesty** with the past – i.e., design for what your organisation needs now and in the future.
2. Design with **"DNA"**. Look at the formal and informal structures in your organisation as you design.
3. Fix the **structure last**, not first.
4. Make the most of top **talent**. Allow flexibility in organisational design for people and personalities – within reason.
5. Focus on what you can **control** – given the regulatory, sector and environmental hand you have been dealt.
6. Promote **accountability** – by clarifying decision-making rights and the boundaries of responsibility.
7. **Benchmark sparingly**, if at all – what worked for another organisation may not work for yours.
8. Let the "lines and boxes" fit your company's **purpose**.
9. Accentuate the **informal**. Structure is not a panacea. Give as much recognition to networks, ways of working and culture.
10. Build on your **strengths**. Find what's good and build on that.

Spans and layers principles say that staff should not have more than around six direct reports and, even for quite large organisations, shouldn't be more than about six layers removed

---

[21] Neilson, Gary L., Jaime Estupiñán, and Bhushan Sethi. "10 Principles of Organization Design." *strategy+business*, March 23, 2015. Accessed May 27, 2017. https://www.strategy-business.com/article/00318?gko=c7329.

from the CEO. Flatter structures promote faster communication, with less risk of the message being garbled. A reasonable number of direct reports allows managers to properly coach and develop their people. However, structure isn't everything and informal ways of working are just as important. Yes, at some point it's good to look at this and encourage people not to have 20 direct reports, or 10 layers beneath them. But only after you have done the other steps above.

Warning signs

An overly static or churning workforce. If attrition levels are too high, this can be a sign of disaffection, bad employee experience, incorrectly set remuneration levels or culture problems. An overly static workforce may mean that the organisation has become staid and cosy, and is lacking in new thought. You want a healthy influx of new people and new ideas, with enough experience and corporate memory to maintain effectiveness.

A high volume of grievances. Reflects staff dissatisfaction and possibly an inability to resolve issues informally. If grievances are clustered in a particular area of the organisation, that merits investigation.

Cultural issues, either expressly stated or implied.

Collective bargaining / union issues. An unhappy relationship with the union hampers the organisation and indicates something isn't working well in employee relations.

A pattern in exit interviews. What's causing your people to leave? How much attrition is regretted? Are there themes?

Good to great

Once the hygiene factors are sorted, how can high-performing HR teams drive forward the performance of the organisation?

Culture and engagement. Owned by all but often steered by HR. HR should be plugged into the culture of the organisation, cultivating the things that are strong and positive, and coming up with plans to address the negatives.

Integrated talent and succession planning. This is the end-to-end process of talent management: assessing needs, identifying high-potential employees, calling out gaps in succession and managing and rotating high-performance individuals. When used in conjunction with strategic position management (going beyond people to capabilities), it provides a strong basis for workforce planning to underpin the strategy.

HR analytics and the "datafication" of HR. A big and untapped area, analytics is becoming an increasing focus for forward-thinking HR managers. Data can transform our ability to connect with and to manage people. HR information systems can put huge amounts of data into HR's hands about absence, performance, productivity, etc. Smart HR departments will analyse this goldmine and use it to get the best out of their people. This has the opportunity to do for HR what it does for Finance – give HR a strategic seat at the executive table, with rich insight backed by quantitative metrics.

Current hot topics

Performance management – abandoning the annual appraisal. The benefits of the annual performance appraisal process are being hotly contested at the moment, with some organisations throwing out the annual process in favour of training managers to become better on-the-job coaches, with regular performance discussions taking place as part of business as usual.

Organisational design. Organisational design needs to take into account new ways of working, new digital technologies, new roles and new attitudes. Far beyond moving "sticks and boxes" diagrams, this is (almost) doing away with sticks and boxes altogether in favour of agile, networked teams focused on delivery of specific projects.

Flexible / agile / SMART working. Employees are looking for flexibility but also for guidance and direction on what's acceptable as the new norm and what's not. Managers need guidance in this strange, new world of working. Staff also want their processes and technology to support new ways of working.

A kickback against process in favour of a better people experience. A growing expectation that HR policies and systems should work for people rather than dictate inflexible processes.

How to engage and keep the millennials. Whether all the characterisations of millennials are fair or not, what's clear is that the implicit contract with this new generation is entirely different, and organisations are struggling to keep up.

Employee wellbeing. Progressive organisations are paying a lot of attention to the areas of wellness and mindfulness. These are important areas of current research – how to help people and organisations adjust to change, how to support them in managing increasingly difficult work / life balance challenges, and how to help them learn and develop in ways that challenge traditional training methods.

Diversity. Diversity in its broadest sense now goes beyond the traditional areas of age, gender and sexual orientation. This extends to giving consideration to reintegration of working parents, the need to care for elders and normalising conversations about mental health. A specific new requirement for gender pay gap reporting – officially reporting on the differences between what men and women in the organisation are paid – is an important concern for HR.

Diversity

Diversity is about increasing value contribution by bringing together people with a wide range of perspectives and experiences.

Competencies. It's generally recognised now that capabilities and competencies are often better indicators of success than specific knowledge, background or skills (see *Good to Great: Why Some Companies Make the Leap and Others Don't* by Jim Collins). Having a competency framework that consciously seeks to develop the right competencies for the organisation is a much more enlightened way of looking at people development than looking at what exact tasks they performed in their last role.

Succession planning. What are your critical roles? Who will succeed the people who are in them currently? Are successors being developed and mentored? Most organisations still don't do this very well.

Apprenticeships, internships and work placement. A hot topic in the UK at the moment. Organisations with a payroll over £3m have to pay an apprenticeship levy to the government, which can then be used to pay for apprenticeships.

Employee Value Proposition ("EVP"). How well does your organisation know what attracts, motivates and retains the employees it wants? Remuneration is often surprisingly low down the list, and yet it's often all that Management talk about. Looking across the multi-dimensional aspects of the employee experience and tailoring the employee experience to what matters to people will pay dividends.

Extract of an EVP I drafted for Save the Children

This all comes down to talent. Great talent will build great systems and processes. If we are to succeed, we need to attract the brightest thinkers to build our platform. We can't pay what they would be paid elsewhere, so we have to develop an unbeatable employee value proposition and broadcast it to where the best people are.

The **Employee Value Proposition** should include elements such as:

- The opportunity to learn and accelerate your career here, faster than anywhere else
- Feeling absolutely great about what you do

- Enjoying a freer, more empowered experience
- The ability to talk to your family about what you do, and bring them in to your work
- Benefiting from a positive perception of the time you spend in the NGO sector
- Regardless of what you have done before, and what you will do after, knowing that your most important life's work will take place here
- When you join and after you leave, you become part of a global network of alumni, part of a family of brilliant, principled, decent people, who are making the world a better place for children

Practical applications of this could include:

- A genuine sense of connectivity to a great cause, and clear line of sight between one's own work and delivery of our vision for children
- Fluid and flexible working arrangements
- A genuine "smart working" culture, with a flexible, high quality work experience, both in the office and away, supported by enthusiastic line managers who value outcomes and success, not hours spent at a desk
- Self-service systems, making it easy to get things done
- A laptop / iPad culture
- Access to high quality training, content, coaching and mentoring
- A PR strategy that talks about the cutting-edge work we are doing, which boosts our profile
- A range of partnering, secondments and rotation options

- The availability of agile platforms to rapidly develop and test solutions
- Access / tangible proximity to the "front line" of what we do

Checklist of policies

- Staff hiring policy, including background checks and vetting
- Rewards and benefits policy
- Equality and diversity policy
- Employee grievance policy
- Disciplinary policy
- Training policy
- Performance management policy
- Staff loans policy
- Maternity / parental leave policy
- Other leave policies, e.g., compassionate leave, sick leave
- Holiday policy
- Flexible working policy
- Redundancy policy

Ten questions to ask of HR

1. What is the headcount profile of the organisation? Numbers, locations, fixed vs. variable, gender balance?
2. How is talent identified, reviewed and coached?
3. How is the organisation structured (teams, spans, layers)? When was structure last reviewed? When were succession plans last reviewed?
4. What is the leadership style of the Executive team?

5. What is the organisation's learning and capability plan?
6. How does the organisation build a high-performance culture?
7. How is performance measured, assessed and acted upon? What is rewarded and how?
8. What are the hiring, retention and attrition rates across the organisation and at departmental levels?
9. Are employee engagement surveys done? What did the last one say?
10. What do compensation structures look like at all levels of the organisation?

Further reading

Adams, L.: "HR Disrupted: It's time for something different"

Collins, J.: "Good to Great: Why Some Companies Make the Leap and Others Don't"

Ulrich, D.: "HR from the outside in: Six competencies for the future of Human Resources", 2012

"Competence and competence frameworks." Crowe Associates

Gary L. Neilson, Jaime Estupiñán and Bhushan Sethi. "10 Principles of Organization Design." *strategy+business* https://www.strategy-business.com/article/00318?gko=c7329.

"The Changing Role of the CHRO." *Harvard Business Review*

"Predictions for 2017: Everything Is Becoming Digital." *Bersin by Deloitte (paid resource)*

8. Operations

What this department does

Although the term "Operations" has as many different meanings are there are organisations, at its core it's the task of converting inputs into outputs and of creating value for the customer. It's the alchemy by which your product or service is made and delivered— the completion of processes to specified levels of quality. Operations also includes forecasting, capacity planning, scheduling and inventory management.

What "Operations" means in different contexts

Industry	Examples of "operations" functions
Financial services	Customer service, payments, transaction processing, shareholder actions
Transport, e.g., airlines	Reservations, fleet management, flight scheduling, airport assistance, baggage handling
Retail	Shop floor management, order fulfilment, shipping, customer service
Humanitarian organisations	Supporter care, processing of donations, management of mailing lists, staff deployment, running of programmes
Healthcare	Clinical trials, drug manufacture
Extractive industries	Exploration, drilling, container management, storage
Hospitality sector	Hotel room booking, housekeeping, concierge services

Telecommunications	Customer subscriptions, account management, billing, customer service
Food production and processing	Food production lines, canning and packaging
Utilities	Customer billing, payments processing

To be an effective COO, you must have a strong appreciation of the workings of your industry. This means knowing:

- Where your organisation sits in the value chain;
- The challenges and pitfalls both upstream in procurement and downstream, in marketing and distribution;
- The partners and stakeholders who are key to the creation of your products and services;
- The end-to-end processes, their vulnerable points and how quality is being built in.

Detailed frameworks, policies and procedures exist for every industry sector. However, there are operations and quality management principles that are applicable across most sectors, and that is what I focus on here.

Roles and responsibilities

- **Product and service design**. Working with Sales and Marketing on product specifications, manufacturing processes and customer experience.
- **Location of facilities / staff**. Looking strategically at the optimal locations for operations staff – nearshore and far shore – taking cost, availability of skills, language and proximity to supply chain into account.

- **Volume forecasting** and ensuring sufficient capacity. Taking inputs from sales and forecasting workload, volumes and staffing.
- **Supply chain – demand management**. Working with the supply chain team to ensure timely delivery of inputs. In service industries, knowing the times of peak demand from customers (e.g., when banking calls are going to hit their peak).
- **New product sign-off.** Assessing whether a new product or service can be produced, maintained and serviced to an acceptable level of quality and at the right cost.

> Operations should always play a key role in new product sign-off. Whether it's a new drug, mobile phone or credit product, Operations staff need to understand the product's characteristics in precise detail, and be confident that they can deliver to the specifications.

- **Process design**. Creating a step-by-step product manufacturing process or step-by-step service process guidelines (e.g., to walk customers through a new loan / hotel reservation).
- **Scheduling**. Scheduling and timing product runs, staffing schedules, maintenance and down time.
- **Monitoring and reporting**. Monitoring throughput, volumes, incidents, numbers of calls waiting, number of batch jobs completed, etc.
- **Incident management**. Dealing with a faulty batch, system outage or machine failure. Taking the production line

down, resolving the issue and bringing the line on stream again.

- **Quality management**. True quality gets built in rather than inspected out. Quality management includes product design, process simplification and parts specification, as well as instilling a quality culture and quality assurance processes.

Overlaps

Operations will work with the Supply Chain team on the sourcing of inputs to the manufacturing process.

Operations needs to have an ongoing conversation with Sales & Marketing to predict demand.

Operations should have a strong voice around the table when dealing with Sales and R&D (Research & Development) on product and service design.

Finally, in making the best decisions on where to house Operations staff for optimal efficiency and effectiveness, Operations needs a good working relationship with Facilities management.

Relationships to watch

It's common for Operations staff to get bulldozed over when they voice concerns about new products or services being too complex. The Sales & Marketing and R&D teams come up with a dazzling offering that's going to change the market. Operations point out that it has too many moving parts, that the customer journey doesn't make sense, that they can't support so many attributes – and everybody wonders why, six months later, customer complaints are through the roof. As COO you'll have to bridge the disagreements between the optimistic and pessimistic elements of the organisation. One of the best and the least controversial ways to do this is to have a rigorous new product sign-off process which replaces some of the objectivity with firm criteria for assessment of the new idea.

Industry frameworks

Every sector has its own standards by which it designs, maintains and executes its operations. The common theme across all of them is quality.

ISO 9000 is the global standard for Quality Management and Quality Assurance, and the most recognised quality framework for operations to adhere to. There are seven Quality Management Principles (QMPs):

- **QMP 1 – Customer focus.** Quality begins with the customer. Organisations should listen to the voice of the customer to understand their needs and build products and services to meet them.

> **Do customers always know best?**
>
> Organisations such as Apple might argue that customers don't know what they want until it's given to them. This may be true for completely new, innovative products. But for those of us not blessed with the creative genius of Steve Jobs, it's a good idea to check in with our customers to make sure we're giving them what they want.

- **QMP 2 – Leadership.** It is the role of leadership to set the conditions for quality to be achieved.
- **QMP 3 – Engagement of people.** Organisations are made of people. To build quality at all stages of operations, an organisation must engage its people in all stages of the production process.
- **QMP 4 – Process approach.** Quality is best achieved when a process-driven approach is taken at all stages of operations.
- **QMP 5 – Improvement.** Continuous learning and improvement should be a feature of all high-quality operations.
- **QMP 6 – Evidence-based decision making.** Decisions regarding operations should be made rationally, on the basis of sound data.
- **QMP 7 – Relationship management.** An organisation and its suppliers and distributers are mutually dependent and co-exist for the purposes of creating quality.

Whether or not your organisation plans to get the ISO 9000 accreditation, take time to discuss the framework of quality management with your Head of Operations. In practice, many organisations will leverage elements of these frameworks and tailor them to their own environments.

Other quality approaches include **Six Sigma** and **Lean.** Six Sigma is a highly analytical process that seeks to minimise defects via root cause analysis by removing causes of variable quality. It has a range of project methodologies and tools to support both new products and the ongoing production of existing ones. Six Sigma specifically identifies the role of executive leadership in the framework – the COO and others are responsible for setting the overall direction and the vision for quality, empowering people in the organisation to fulfil their roles by breaking down internal siloes and facilitating change management.

Quality management

According to Wikipedia, "Quality management ensures that an organization, product or service is consistent. It has four main components: quality planning, quality assurance, quality control and quality improvement. Quality management is focused not only on product and service quality, but *also on the means to achieve it*. Quality management, therefore, uses quality assurance and control of processes as well as products to achieve more consistent quality."

The dimensions of quality

ISO 9001 Dimensions of Product Quality[22]

- **Performance** – main characteristics of the product
- **Aesthetics** – appearance, feel, smell, taste
- **Special features** – extra characteristics
- **Conformance** – how well the product conforms to design specifications
- **Reliability** – consistency of performance
- **Durability** – the useful life of the product
- **Perceived quality** – indirect evaluation of quality
- **Serviceability** – handling of complaints or repairs

ISO 9001 Dimensions of Service Quality

- **Convenience** –the availability and accessibility of the service
- **Reliability** – ability to perform a service dependably, consistently, and accurately
- **Responsiveness** – willingness to help customers in unusual situations and to deal with problems
- **Time** – the speed with which the service is delivered
- **Assurance** – knowledge exhibited by personnel and their ability to convey trust and confidence
- **Courtesy** – the way customers are treated by employees
- **Tangibles** – the physical appearance of facilities, equipment, personnel, and communication materials

---

[22] "Operations management." Wikipedia. Accessed May 28, 2017 https://en.wikipedia.org/wiki/Operations_management.

> - **Consistency** – the ability to provide the same level of good quality repeatedly

How organisations can boost quality

Operations and quality management may be highly complex topics. When talking to your Head of Operations, you can use the following concepts to broker a conversation about improving quality:

1. Better, regular, real-time engagement with customers. Are there other ways to hear the voice of the customer? Where appropriate, could customers be involved in the design process in order to improve products and make them more responsive to their needs?
2. Design simplicity. Are there too many moving parts in your products or services? Which attributes could be pared back to simplify the design without overly compromising functionality? Which product or service attributes cause Operations the most headaches?
3. Process simplicity. Is the build / servicing process as streamlined as it could be? What are the extraneous steps? What would you do if you could build the process from scratch, unencumbered by legacy processes and ways of working? What would a new entrant do?
4. Involving suppliers in design process. They may have ideas your organisation hasn't thought of.

Involving suppliers in design

The makers of Gü desserts realised that customers were keeping the glass jars their products came in and re-using them. The initial design of the jars didn't allow for them to easily stack – the top of the jar needed to be changed to make it stackable. Initially, the supplier of the jars was unwilling to change its design for a small start-up. However, once Gü started ordering jars by the hundreds of thousands, the supplier was happy to make the change and improve the product.

5. Involving Operations staff in design and assessment. Too often, organisations leave some of the most important stakeholders out of the design process – the Operations staff who will have to make and service the product offering in the real world. How involved are your Operations staff? Could they be brought further into design discussions?

6. Good old-fashioned checklists. This may seem a very simplistic addition, but the use of checklists has transformed Operations in sectors from medicine to banking.

The use of checklists[23]

A professor at Johns Hopkins University wrote an article in The New Yorker about the transformative power of checklists in the Intensive Care Unit. We invited him to Barclays Wealth to discuss how the procedures used in ICU could be leveraged to improve the reliability of banking operations. He told us how the simple rigour of using a reliable, repeatable checklist yielded incredible results in patient safety and recovery, and reduced operational incidents by a significant factor. However, it must be accompanied by a culture of acceptance and openness - junior staff must feel empowered to speak up to their seniors. If a junior nurse picks up on an oversight, they should feel able to challenge the surgeon. We were able to use this insight to strengthen our banking and customer services processes.

Warning signs in Operations

- **A large range of products, not justified by sales figures.** This reflects a lack of rigour between Sales and Operations and an unwillingness to review product ranges and to shut down the underperforming products.
- Large numbers of **defects / broken processes / customer complaints.** Particularly if the same issues are repeating, and the Operations teams don't appear to be learning.

---

[23] "Safety Checklist Use Yields 10 Percent Drop in Hospital Deaths." *John Hopkins Medicine*

Operations regularly being **surprised** by high or low volumes of demand and / or **inputs not being available** when needed. This means demand forecasting isn't working.

- Overly **inflexible processes** and the inability to customise. This reflects the lack of agility in the manufacturing process and can seriously frustrate the Sales team. A lack of front-line empowerment can be particularly de-motivating for call centre staff dealing with irate customers.

- Overly **loose processes** – which can be error-prone and are expensive to maintain. This may be okay and even necessary in the early stages of development of a product or service while the customer needs are understood. However, over time the optionality should be pared back in the interests of efficiency and quality.

- Large amounts of **unscheduled downtime** due to system failures. This reflects a lack of quality management, maintenance, investment or understanding.

Good to great

Apart from quality, the other big watchword in Operations continues to be efficiency. This isn't new, but new ways to achieve efficiency are constantly being developed. The use of big data to predict seasonal variations and to hedge or plan against them is one example. Forecasting demand allows Operations to prepare optimally and avoid needless effort.

For example, in the energy sector, demand modelling and forecasting allows energy providers and consumers to create correlations between variables to predict demand and to gear up their operations accordingly[24]. Big and clever, this work is still in its embryonic stage and has a long way to go.

Current hot topics

Sustainability. Increasingly important to customers and organisations. This involves looking at what impact a product or service has on the environment over its entire life cycle, from the sourcing of raw materials to disposal. It also includes making the manufacturing process as efficient as possible to minimise waste. Linked to this is the possibility of up-cycling / re-cycling / re-using products in different ways. See the Procurement and Corporate Social Responsibility chapters for more on this.

Product innovation / Minimum Viable Product. Organisations are increasingly called upon to innovate. Those that can come up with base case ideas, test them rapidly, learn, pivot and move forward are the ones that will win. Central to this is the concept of the minimum viable product – the most basic version of a potential new product that can be created as quickly and as cheaply as possible to test it out with customers. In *The Idea in You: How to Find It, Build It, and Change Your Life*, authors Martin Amor and Alex Pellew describe how the MVP (Minimum Viable Product) for Innocent Smoothies was homemade smoothies poured into cleaned-out water bottles and distributed for free to commuters

---

[24]https://www.researchgate.net/publication/286649971_Big_data_driven_smart_energy_management_From_big_data_to_big_insights

in Waterloo station in return for customer feedback. One batch of smoothies probably cost around £50 to produce. The learning from the exercise was priceless.

Globalisation / localisation. Linked to sustainability is a renewed thoughtfulness about where products are sourced. Small-batch, craft and artisan products are increasingly popular. In addition, there has been a recent kickback against globalisation of late, particularly in the UK and US, with an increasing focus on national protection.

Agility. The ability to adapt quickly to changing customer needs. For example, the clothing chain Zara now has new intakes of garments *several times a month* into its stores. Gone are the days of the Spring / Summer and Autumn / Winter collections!

AI (Artificial Intelligence) / predictive modelling. Most forward-leaning organisations have at least a few maths geeks, if not entire departments, charged with using techniques to predict demand in ever more clever ways.

The use of predictive modelling

Amazon pre-positions supplies, guessing what we're going to order before we know we want it. The fundraising website JustGiving claims to know, better than we do, how much money we're going to raise by analysing the characteristics of our Facebook friends. Imagine the possibilities for the world if that kind of modelling could be used to predict the next drought or the next outbreak of cholera and pre-position supplies in just the right place.

Cost control. In these straitened times, there is a consistent focus on simply getting cost out of the system. Some organisations are willing to forego some functionality and features in favour of cost reduction. As COO, this is often a key part of your brief.

Ten questions to ask

Ten questions to ask of Operations

1. What volumes of production – both current and historic – are being supported?
2. Operational incidents. What are the error rates as a percentage of operations performed? What is the trend? What are the drivers of the errors?
3. What outsourcing relationships do we have in place?
4. Who are our major suppliers? What are relationships like with them?
5. How are operational problems escalated and resolved?
6. When was operations last audited? What was the auditor's opinion?
7. Describe the technology systems supporting end-to-end operations. Is it an integrated system? What are the key interfaces? Where are the weak points?
8. How is consistency of quality ensured across different Operations sites?
9. What volume of customer complaints is received every month? What are the themes? What has been the trend?
10. What are the volumes of calls into the call centres? What are the most common queries or issues? How do we

engage with customers to hear their voices and to get their views?

Checklist of policies

- Quality policy
- New product approval and sign-off policy

Further reading

The Idea in You: How to Find It, Build It, and Change Your Life by Martin Amor, Alex Pellew

"Safety Checklist Use Yields 10 Percent Drop in Hospital Deaths." *John Hopkins Medicine*

9. Risk

What this department does

The Risk department is charged with supporting Management in the identification, analysis, evaluation and management of the key risks facing the organisation, and in setting the appropriate risk culture within the organisation. It is part of your *second line of defence* against issues that can derail your strategy and undermine your operations. Most cataclysmic organisational events (the collapse of Barings bank, the Deepwater Horizon oil spill, etc.) happen due to risk management failures.

ISO Guide 73:2009 elegantly defines risk as "the effect of uncertainty on objectives."[25] Your Risk team helps you, the Board and Executive Management to work out what could derail your objectives and what mitigations could prevent it. When your Head of Risk talks – listen. Set the tone for the rest of the organisation to listen too.

Roles and responsibilities

- Creating a Risk taxonomy – defining a common risk language for the organisation.
- Risk identification. Linking to the business strategy and assisting management in the identification of the key risks facing the organisation.

---

[25] "ISO Guide 73:2009." ISO. November 2009. Accessed May 31, 2017. https://www.iso.org/standard/44651.html.

- Assisting management in assessing the likelihood and significance of risks manifesting, so that risks can be scaled, classified and appropriately prioritised.
- Risk mitigation, avoidance, management or acceptance. The Risk team supports Management in devising the appropriate responses to the identified risks.
- Identification, logging and remediation of risk incidents and near-misses. When things go wrong, the Risk team works with Management to identify root causes, making sure people learn the lessons and remediate the identified control weaknesses.
- Control assessments. Supporting Management in assessing the design and operating effectiveness of the control systems. Where there are control weaknesses, recommending improvements via a control enhancement plan.

Residual risk = Inherent risk minus Controls

Design effectiveness: Have the controls been well-designed?

Operating effectiveness: Are the controls operating as designed?

- Horizon scanning. Taking an external, medium to long-range view on the macro changes in the external environment, and looking at what could disrupt the organisation.
- Risk management functions which include:
  - Insurance (can be part of Finance)
  - Business continuity / Disaster recovery planning (can be part of IT)
  - Health, Safety & Security

> **The different types of risk**
>
> - Market risk – the impact of financial market movements on your organisation
> - Credit risk – the risk of those who owe you money not paying as expected
> - Operational risk – the risk of people, systems and processes not operating as expected
> - Liquidity risk – the risk the organisation cannot meet its short-term financial requirements
> - Information security risk – the risk of IT systems being compromised or failing
> - Conduct risk – the risk of people doing the wrong thing
> - Regulatory risk – the risk of falling foul of industry rules and frameworks

Enterprise-wise risk management is the overall framework that supports your organisation to identify, rank, manage and report on its risks. Be aware of the difference between the day-to-day losses in areas such as Operations (where losses are a function of volume and complexity) versus lower frequency but higher impact "tail" risks. Spending your time, energy, focus and investment on the day-to-day losses might yield benefits in the short term, but it won't protect against "tail" risk events. Assessing these will require big, bold decisions and won't be popular – they may never materialise and could cost a lot to protect against.

Lines of defence

Risk management can only be meaningful when every employee plays a role in identifying and managing risks. The days when you could hand risk management over to a separate team to "take care of things" are long gone, to the extent that they ever really existed. In-house Risk professionals will tell you they're only the second line of defence – the first line of defence is Management. Management owns and manages risk. Second-line functions, such as Risk, are responsible for designing frameworks and provide check and challenge to Management. The third line is the Audit function, which independently verifies the organisation's control environment. No single line of defence is sufficient – they operate as an interconnected system.

Management – the first line of defence

Management creates business objectives to further its strategy. It must be cognisant of the risks that could derail the achievement of those objectives. Good risk management means understanding those risks and identifying the strengths and the weaknesses of the controls and the processes in the organisation. Management must set tolerances around what risks it's willing to accept – this is called "setting the risk appetite."

Risk appetite is particularly meaningful in a humanitarian setting. When assessing a new deployment, you know that you are putting your people in harm's way. How do you evaluate the indispensable good that they are doing for weak, vulnerable and dying people, against the risk that some of your staff might not come home?

CASE STUDY: Preparing for Ebola

In 2014, the Ebola pandemic was spreading like wildfire through Sierra Leone and Liberia in West Africa. Deaths, while still in the hundreds, were increasing exponentially. The risk of contagion for those countries, for the continent and for the world was high. Save the Children, along with other agencies, felt they had no choice but to intervene. The UK Ministry of Defence was building a treatment centre in Kerrytown, Sierra Leone. They asked Save the Children UK to run it. Save the Children US took on a similar role in Liberia. The nature of this deployment was like nothing we had experienced before. It was different from going into the aftermath of an earthquake, or even into a warzone. A slip-up in procedures, carelessness in taking off a suit, a small rip in protective gear could result in a grim, horrible death for an aid worker. Their bodies would not be repatriated, and their families would not be able to bury them.

The only way to meet this challenge was honestly and directly. No staff member was to be compelled to take part in this operation - it was entirely voluntary. There was no shame or negative consequence on those who did not participate. We listed the risks and their implications. We encouraged staff to discuss deployment with their loved ones. We mobilised organisational psychologists and made it mandatory for any person considering deployment to have a session with them to ensure they understood the risks and had the mental strength to see the deployment through. We assured people that they could return at any time if they felt they couldn't cope (many of these people had been in humanitarian crises from Ethiopia to Mogadishu, from Darfur to Haiti). We rehearsed and rehearsed. We ensured our robust protocols were communicated, adhered to and role-modelled by everyone – from the CEO to the junior staff. We brought in staff from Public Health England to speak to our London HQ staff about the precautions in place for people returning to the office. We stepped up the cleaning rotation inside the office. Out in the field, we provided the staff with slightly nicer accommodation than usual (not five-star by any means, but a little better than normal) so they could have some much-needed downtime after the horrors they had witnessed. When people returned, they attended mandatory post-deployment counselling and assessment. Humanitarians don't usually ask for help until it's too late and they are struggling with post-traumatic stress disorder. If you make counselling mandatory, there is no shame in people attending.

Preparing for Ebola was the most intense mobilisation I have ever witnessed. It required exceptional cross-function collaborative working. The honesty, the candour and the rigour with which preparations were made was like nothing I had ever seen. Staff signed up, willingly. We saved almost 300 people, gave hundreds more the best treatment possible prior to their sad deaths, and contained the virus. On 7 November 2015, Sierra Leone was pronounced Ebola-free.

When done badly, risk assessment results in tomes of meaningless reports on A3 paper, in 8-point font that twitchy line managers "sign off" once a year. These typically also result in a distorted view of risk, where the number one item is the fact that the business continuity plan hasn't been tested for six months. Don't get me wrong, testing your BCP is important, but if it doesn't gel with what the CEO is worrying about, risk management needs to do better.

Good risk management means Senior Management understanding the risks that matter and building a picture where controls are weak and need enhancement. You can do this by taking both a forward- and a backward-looking view. The backward-looking view involves looking at risk incidents and near-misses that have previously occurred. If you're having repeated incidents in a particular area, this indicates a weakness. Near-misses are often not captured. In almost every major risk incident there are warning signs that could have been heeded. The forward-looking view involves assessing the environment and the variables that could change in the future – "horizon scanning" – then combining that with what is known about the organisation's weak spots, to forecast what could go wrong.

Identifying the near-misses

A few years ago, the NHS (National Health Service) launched a programme designed to encourage the reporting of near-misses, guaranteeing protection for those who reported them. Similarly, in child safeguarding, best practice encourages the reporting of "it's probably nothing, but" concerns – issues that haven't manifested yet but are slightly outside the norm. Caught in time, these minor issues can often be remediated with no blame or sanction attached to either the reporter or

---

> the alleged perpetrator, and avoiding much more significant issues in the future.

Your role as COO, as well as supporting your Risk team, is to cultivate a culture of reporting and of learning. You have to address fear of blame or reprisal, and support those who point out issues. I discuss whistleblowing more in the Legal chapter.

Risk team – the second line of defence

If Management owns Risk, what do you need the Risk department for? The Risk department is responsible for:

- putting a risk framework in place
- providing check and challenge to management assessments
- taking an overall view of the interdependencies of the risk environment
- monitoring and reporting on risk incidents, remediation plans and outstanding risks above risk appetite

Good Risk professionals understand their organisations, the context they operate in, the trends, the disruptive influences and the regulatory context. They can guide Management towards robust assessments of potential problems. Bad Risk managers hide behind process and terminology, fat frameworks and wordy risk assessments. Paperwork is their comfort.

Strong risk managers are prepared to challenge Management appropriately and hold them to account if they feel that the risk frameworks are not effectively deployed, or that the risk culture is not what it needs to be. You need a risk team with spine - and a Risk Director who is not afraid to speak up and be unpopular.

Audit – third line of defence

Internal and external audit are viewed as the third line of defence. These are independent teams, who validate the operation of controls against how the organisation has designed and documented them. They report on exceptions, on processes that don't stand up to scrutiny, and on inconsistencies and failures. The Internal Audit department is concerned with controls and processes, and reports its findings to Management. External Audit is concerned with the truth and fairness of the annual accounts, as well as the reliability of the systems that underpin them. External Audit may rely on some of the findings of internal Audit to determine how much work it needs to do, but the two are separate and serve different aims.

Overlaps

A number of Risk management roles can sit in different areas. Information Security can sit in IT or be a standalone department (it sits best as a subset of Risk). Insurance is sometimes under Finance. Health, Safety & Security might be a standalone department as well.

Relationships to watch

How your CEO and other department heads interact with your Head of Risk will tell you a lot about the risk culture. It may also tell you something about the quality of your Head of Risk. Are they business-savvy? Do they understand your organisation at a deep level? Do they know where the money is made? Where the corners can't be cut? Where there are key weak points? Or are they box-tickers, slavishly implementing standard frameworks?

Organisations get the Risk professionals they deserve. If they take the time to recruit talented people – if they pay them, empower them, listen to them and take action on their recommendations – they'll have a strong Risk team. If they don't take time to recruit carefully, don't incentivise the Head of Risk, pay them lip service and slowly take action against open, identified risks, they'll likely have a demotivated journeyman – and a team to match. You must champion Risk – get the right team in place, show everyone you take Risk seriously, take counsel from your Head of Risk and take action to show you mean business and intend for the organisation to do things in the right way.

Industry frameworks

ISO 30001 is the industry standard for Enterprise Risk Management. It contains the following provisions:

- **Planning and designing.** Writing the Risk Policy, setting the Board mandate and commitment to risk management; defining the roles of the Audit and Risk Committees, the Executive Team, and the Risk Management Team.
- **Implementing and benchmarking.** Performing risk assessments, reviews, analysis and horizon scanning, including looking at the external environment and other players.

- **Measuring and monitoring.** Recording and evaluating risks; evaluating the controls or mitigants that should reduce them; examining risk incidents and understanding why, to avoid them in future.
- **Learning and reporting.** Closing the loop; embedding a culture of ongoing learning and improvement, so that the organisation's considerable investment in risk management actually pays off over time.

Business resilience and Business Continuity Management

Business Continuity Management ("BCM") is a critically important part of risk management that can be overlooked. Different people assign different meanings to disaster recovery vs. business continuity. Here, I'm using it to embrace all aspects of responding to a crisis – from the initial emergency to the long-term resumption of "normal" operations. BCP is subject to its own quality standard – ISO 27001.

As COO, you are accountable for assuring the ongoing functioning of your operations. Assign responsibility for BCM to somebody in the organisation that you trust. At a minimum, they should take the following steps.

- Creation of an **Emergency Incident response plan**. What happens in the immediate aftermath of an emergency (e.g., terror incident, building unavailable, PR crisis)? Who contacts whom? What are their home contact details? Who informs staff what to do, and how? Get these basics down quickly, ensure everyone has a copy at home and walk through it with them, so people know what to do and can mobilise when needed.

- Creation of a **Business Continuity Plan ("BCP")**. The main steps in creating a BCP are below. Your staff may be able to do this themselves. If you're short of expertise or time, you can hire consultants.

  o **Business Impact Analysis.** What critical processes need to be immediately "up" following an incident? What needs to be functioning within 8 hours, 24 hours, 48 hours, one week?

  o **BCM overall strategy.** How is the organisation going to meet the needs above? Can it rely on other locations if one site becomes available? Does it need to pay for hot/warm third party sites? What IT systems need immediate failover? How frequently are system backups required? What people are needed?

  o **Detailed recovery procedures.** Showing what happens when – step by step, team by team, to bring operations back online. These should be designed, written and tested by the people closest to the processes. Don't just think about IT and operational systems. What staff support / counselling services will be available? Who will manage Public Relations?

  o **Long-term continuity planning.** What happens if certain facilities or systems are out of commission for an extended period of time? This is worth considering, but in practice, Management will make some of these decisions in response to events.

- o **Re-integration to business as usual.** This will need to be flexed dependent on circumstances. You will need a staged process to restore operations to normal following an incident.

- **Communication.** How will staff be made aware of their responsibilities – both *before* an incident happens and *while* it occurs? What if the crisis takes place outside of working hours? Mapping out training, awareness and communications.

- **Learning / resilience / near misses / incident response.** When a false fire alarm goes off, when there's a facilities problem, when someone gets stuck in an elevator – are your teams using these events to learn and to enhance systems and controls?

- Working with **local authorities and other bodies**. The staff charged with BCP responsibility should be plugged into the appropriate local authorities – fire, police and counter-terrorism – so they receive timely updates and have open lines of communication, should the need arise.

- **Ongoing maintenance and review.** Plans don't stay fresh for long. Your Head of BCM should design a way to get them checked and refreshed periodically. Regular, low-impact updates are best.

Typical monthly Risk report content:

The Executive Team should be discussing risk as an intrinsic part of all its discussions. In addition, on at least a monthly basis it's good to take stock of the risk environment. A report from your Risk team to Management should contain the following elements:

- Headlines / executive summary
- Changes in environment/context – external events that pose new risks or opportunities
- Key new / increasing risks
- Risk events during this period; lessons-learned analysis, including control issues identified by Management
- Risks closed out or reduced to within tolerance
- Risks plotted on a dashboard, ranked by significance and likelihood, with explanations for their ranking; headline action to be taken with a date against it.
- Audits open, closed and in progress, and their findings
- Number of open and overdue audit points

Warning signs

- Risks that change little – quarter by quarter, year by year. This is a sign of a stale, overly theoretical framework not linked to the strategy, or risks that have been defined over too large a scope and too long a timescale.
- Risk frameworks that are overly theoretical, hard to understand and full of jargon. I always look for risks to be spelled out in plain English and to hit you right between the eyes.
- Dissonance between what your Risk team is telling you to worry about and what you really worry about. This indicates either that the Risk team is not sufficiently

plugged into what makes the organisation tick, or that Management doesn't have the appropriate attitude to risk.

- Risks that recur – a strong risk framework will capture risk events when they occur, understand the root cause and take action to ensure that particular issue doesn't arise again. If risks are recurring, then your organisation isn't learning from them.

- A culture that ignores, or pays lip service to, risk management – form over substance.

- A culture where risk is passed to the Risk team, where there is an overdependence on a "parent" telling people things are okay: "The Head of Risk has signed this off and said it's okay, so I guess it's okay". Management has to own its risks.

- External Audit performing large amounts of substantive testing (which costs you money), because they feel they can't rely on the organisational controls that are supposed to be in place.

- Large numbers of internal audit reports of weak findings.

- Large numbers of open and overdue audit points. This is always a bugbear of mine.

> **No excuse for overdue audit actions**
>
> At the conclusion of an audit, individual managers agree to complete audit actions to remediate the control weaknesses that have been identified. They usually get to agree there is a risk and decide the remediation action, who will be responsible for it, and the timeline. If, having

agreed the action, the manager doesn't see through this commitment, this means one of several things:

- They got the action wrong
- They underestimated the time required for the fix
- They didn't prioritise the fix
- They didn't think through the dependencies of the fix
- They never thought it was important in the first place and just agreed with it for a quiet life

Whichever of the above reasons it was, it doesn't paint a very good picture. I am always maniacally simple about audit actions and remediation of control issues: If a manager doesn't agree it's a high priority problem, they should say so and explain why. If they're not capable of thinking through dependencies or estimating a reasonable timeline (with contingency built in), then how competent are they? If it is high priority and they haven't prioritised fixing it, then what does that say about them?

- Business continuity plans that haven't been tested
- A high number of operational risk incidents

Good to great

Once the operational aspects of Risk are going well, you can challenge your Risk team to help embed risk in the culture of the organisation. Your organisation is properly embracing risk management when:

- It's no longer viewed as the role of the Risk team to manage risk.
- Risk is embodied in the language of the organisation.
- Risks are analysed, in real time, at the early concept stage of new ideas. Safeguards are dynamically built in, almost without people thinking about it. Built in instead of inspected out. Forward-looking instead of backward.

You have a great risk culture when your Risk staff are viewed as helpful experts to provide check and challenge, but risk is ultimately owned by each person, manager, department head and the CEO.

Risk is going well when risk event monitoring and mitigation have led to meaningful improvements in the quality of your processes. As a result of this processes will run more seamlessly, with less outages, less defects, less friction and greater employee satisfaction.

Current hot topics

General Data Protection Regulation ("GDPR"). The GDPR was agreed in April 2016 and will come into effect in May 2018. It proposes sweeping changes in the approach to personal data, and raises the sanctions for non-compliance to greater heights.

The **EU Network and Information Security Directive** was agreed in December 2015. It requires member states to be prepared and equipped to respond to security incidents. It requires providers of "essential services" such as energy companies, banks and healthcare providers to take appropriate security measures and notify serious incidents to the authorities.

Data quality and lineage. Understanding where your data is sourced from and ensuring its timeliness and accuracy.

Cyber security. Approximately half of all FTSE 350 companies regard cyber-attacks as their single biggest risk[26]. I include this risk here rather than in the Information Technology chapter because it's more pervasive across the organisation and isn't confined to IT.

Three risks under Cyber security:

- Data loss through hacking
- Financial loss through theft
- Operational failures (e.g., due to denial of service attacks)

Technical developments, increased regulation, greater sophistication on the part of the bad guys, and the increasing reliance of organisations on technology are all contributing to making this a melting pot of risk, that your Executive team and Board should be concerned about. Your role is to give this issue sufficient airtime, promote awareness and resource your Risk and Technology teams appropriately to counter the risk.

Business resilience. BCP often focuses on IT recovery. Resilience looks more broadly at property, IT, suppliers and people, and examines business resilience in a more integrated and holistic

---

[26] "FTSE 350 Cyber Governance Health Check Report 2015." GOV.UK. 2016. Accessed June 3, 2017.
https://www.gov.uk/government/uploads/system/uploads/attachment_data/file/521484/Cyber_Governance_Health_Check_report_2015.pdf.

way. Progressive organisations are performing sophisticated scenario mapping and examining the effects of scenarios on their resilience.

Outsourcing processes and the associated risk implications. This isn't new but is receiving a lot of focus at the current time due to an increased interest in outsourcing to achieve cost efficiency.

Checklist of risk policies

- Overall risk policy and framework; setting out roles and responsibilities and containing risk appetite
- Insurance policy – what you insure against and self-insurance
- Whistleblowing policy
- Child / vulnerable person safeguarding policy (if applicable)
- Background checks policy (HR)
- Vetting of customers / suppliers policy

Ten questions to ask about Risk

1. Is there a defined risk framework (roles & responsibilities, policy, thresholds, definitions, governance)?
2. Is there a formal Risk Committee? Who sits on it and what is its remit? Does it have meaningful discussions on risks and responses?
3. Is there a risk register containing the key risks, ranked by significance and likelihood? Does it make sense to you when you read it alongside the business plan?

4. Is there a detailed set of risks and corresponding controls? Are the controls well-designed to cover the risks? Are they tested and verified on a periodic basis?

5. Do risk incidents / near-misses get captured? Do the root causes get followed up and rectified by fixing a process or by putting in place additional training? Is there a formal lessons learned process?

6. What's the culture of Risk in the organisation? What kind of attitude is displayed by staff regarding risk – is it risk averse or cavalier? Is risk seen as a tick box exercise, or does it inform decision making?

7. What is the calibre of the Risk team? Are they people with deep knowledge of the organisation? Do they know where the skeletons are buried? Or are they "phoning it in," blindly applying fancy frameworks that mean very little? Do you agree with their view of the key risks - are they the same risks that keep you up at night?

8. Who are the Internal and External auditors? How long have they been in place? What do they say about the organisation?

9. How is customer / client data confidentiality maintained? Is the organisation ready for GDPR?

10. What is the organisation doing about business resilience? What are the Disaster Recovery / Business Continuity arrangements? Where is the plan? When was it last tested? What is the role of the COO in it?

Further reading

A structured approach to Enterprise Risk Management (ERM) and the requirements of ISO 31000:
https://www.theirm.org/media/886062/ISO3100_doc.pdf

10. GOVERNANCE

What this department does

Governance may or may not be a separate department in your organisation – it may be the responsibility of Legal or Risk – but good governance, however achieved, is integral to the functioning of your organisation. Governance as a concept determines how an organisation make decisions and how the Executive and Non-Executive departments interact with one another to direct and oversee the organisation.

Good governance is often invisible or taken for granted. Organisations sometimes get away with weak governance for a period of time, but it almost always comes back to bite them. A COO who allows governance to grow weak is rarely forgiven. Although a number of key responsibilities fall to the Board and other Executives, it's the COO and their Compliance, Risk and Legal staff who are expected to concern themselves with good governance.

Roles and responsibilities

The role of Governance is to design a hierarchy of decision-making powers, ensuring checks and balances, and adequate segregation of duties. The key bodies that make decisions at the top of an organisation are usually the following:

- **Board of Trustees** ("the Board"). The body with the overall legal responsibility for an organisation. If the organisation is publicly listed, the Board is appointed to act on behalf of the shareholders to safeguard their needs and ensure the overall success of the organisation. The Board has ultimate responsibility for setting the vision, mission and values of the organisation, as well as the strategy. It delegates the day to day responsibility to Management but retains the responsibility for oversight of performance.

The following boards or sub-committees assist the Board in discharging its responsibilities.

- **The Finance Committee, including the Pensions Committee.** The Finance Committee oversees the finances of the organisation. Its responsibilities include oversight of sales, income, fundraising, expenditure, cash flow, treasury, reserves and the financial control environment. If there is a separate Pensions Committee, it is charged with the guardianship of the organisation's pension fund, for the good of the plan's members.
- **Audit Committee.** Audit Committees are charged with oversight of the Internal and External audit functions of an organisation. Typically, they are also responsible for oversight of the organisation's control environment. They, and not the Finance Committee, sign off the annual accounts, reflecting the importance of the control environment in assuring the numbers. They appoint and remove the external auditors.

> **Audit Committee responsibilities:**
>
> - Monitoring the control environment, systems, processes, internal audit and risk management
> - Monitoring the financial reporting process
> - Overseeing the statutory audit
> - Appointing and removing the External Auditor

- **Risk Committee.** The Risk Committee is responsible for oversight of the organisation's risk management framework, challenging the Executive to identify all the relevant risks that might be facing the organisation and establish appropriate risk management to deal with those risks.

- **Remuneration Committee.** The Remuneration Committee is responsible for the overall remuneration and reward structure in the organisation, including executive remuneration. It considers what performance factors influence remuneration, assesses the performance of the CEO and determines what reporting disclosures should be made about remuneration in the Annual Report.

- **Nominations and appointments.** The Nominations Committee considers the skills and capabilities that are required on the Board of Trustees and sets the terms for Trustee appointment, reconsideration and retirement. It's usually involved in the recruitment of the CEO, COO and other executive roles.

- **Risk and reputation, sustainability, corporate social responsibility.** There may be additional committees tasked with overseeing sustainability and stewarding the organisation's legacy and reputation.

Overlaps and relationships to watch

These committees can work in a number of different ways:

- The Audit and Risk Committees can be subsumed into one.
- The Pensions Committee may or may not be separate from the Finance Committee.
- Remuneration and nominations may be handled by the Board.

As a new-in-role COO, you'll be interested in how the committees have been set up, what is working well and what could be improved. Asking both your Executive and Non-Executive colleagues about this will give you a lot of insight. Bear in mind, there are usually drawbacks in whatever structure is chosen, so it's rarely perfect. It is acceptable, even expected, that a new COO will challenge the current setup. Just make sure that it's not challenge for the sake of it, and that you have a clear rationale for the alternatives you are proposing.

The Audit Committee should have a direct line of access to the Board, bypassing the Executive departments, so they can escalate concerns directly if required. It's also good practice for the Internal Audit Department to have a direct line of access to the Audit Committee for escalation purposes.

The interplay of all these committees with the Board is critical to the organisation's success, as is the interaction between the Executive and Non-Executive functions. A Board that is too hands-off and theoretical is going to struggle to properly oversee the organisation. One that is too engaged in the day-to-day decision-making will frustrate the executives and lead to analysis paralysis.

The role of the COO on Non-Executive Committees

As a newly-appointed COO, you are likely to have a role on some or all of these committees. This may be a new experience for you. How you establish your relationship with your Board members will be a key determinant of your success. A few key tips to assist with your preparation:

- Get to know the details – both financial and operational. In particular, you will likely be expected to report on delivery of the organisation's strategy.
- Try to meet some key Board members in advance of the set meetings to gauge their areas of concern.
- Work with your Executive colleagues on the outline of the Board session in advance. Who should speak in each section? Should it be a presentation or on paper? What are going to be the hot questions from the individual Board members? Who should answer them? You can't manage for every eventuality, but a little advance choreography goes a long way.
- Know the boundaries of the Executive and Non-Executive functions. If you feel the meeting is going down a detailed rabbit-hole, gently bring it back up.
- Get the Non-Executives involved, appropriately, in the workings of the organisation. What skills do they have? Can they bring some of their experience and frameworks to bear?

They may welcome the opportunity to get involved and be more supportive as a result.

- Be ready to discuss the key risks and the mitigations the organisation has against them.
- Don't bluff. Ever. But you know that.

Industry frameworks

The key framework for Governance in the UK is the UK Corporate Governance Code[27]. It has five main principles, summarised below;

Leadership. "Every company should be headed by an effective Board, with division of responsibilities between the Board and the Executive... No one individual should have unfettered powers of decision."

Effectiveness. "The Board and its committees should have the appropriate balance of skills, experience, independence and knowledge of the company to ... discharge their respective duties and responsibilities effectively."

Accountability. "The Board should present a fair, balanced and understandable assessment of the company's position and prospects... The Board should maintain sound risk management and internal control systems."

---

[27] https://www.frc.org.uk/Our-Work/Publications/Corporate-Governance/UK-Corporate-Governance-Code-April-2016.pdf

Remuneration "There should be a formal and transparent procedure for ... fixing the remuneration packages of individual directors ... No director should be involved in deciding his or her own remuneration."

Relations with shareholders. "There should be a dialogue with shareholders based on the mutual understanding of objectives."

There is a voluntary good governance code for the Voluntary and Community sector[28], which has six principles, with further explanation of good practice. The headlines are that an effective Board will provide good governance and leadership by:

1. Understanding their role
2. Ensuring delivery of the organisation's purpose
3. Working effectively, both as individuals and as a team
4. Exercising effective control
5. Behaving with integrity
6. Being open and accountable

Charity Commission Guidance Note 26[29] also talks about governance risks, including the risk of inappropriate organisational structure, the risk that the Trustees lack the relevant skills or commitment and the risk of conflicts of interest.

In the US, two sets of principles of Corporate Governance have come out in the recent past – the *Commonsense Principles of*

---

[28] http://www.governancecode.org/code_versions/. Note the code is currently under revision
[29] https://www.gov.uk/government/publications/charities-and-risk-management-cc26/charities-and-risk-management-cc26

Corporate Governance[30] and the *Corporate Governance Principles for US Listed Companies*[31]. Both are voluntary, and organisations appear to be signing up to one or the other. Both sets of principles speak to the need for competent directors with high levels of integrity to represent the needs of shareholders. Both cover Board self-assessment and the need for turnover of members. Neither have sanctions for failure to comply. Time will tell if these become generally accepted, if one wins out over the other, and whether a voluntary code is going to be sufficient.

Commonsense principles	Investor Stewardship Group Principles for US listed companies
Board of Directors • Composition • Election of Directors • Nominating Directors • Director compensation and stock ownership • Board committee structure and service • Director tenure and retirement age • Director effectiveness	Principle 1: Boards are accountable to shareholders

[30] http://www.governanceprinciples.org/wp-content/uploads/2016/07/GovernancePrinciples_Principles.pdf

[31] https://www.isgframework.org/corporate-governance-principles/

Board of Directors' responsibilities	Principle 2: Shareholders should be entitled to voting rights in proportion to their economic interest
• Director communication with third parties • Critical activities of the board; setting the agenda • Shareholder rights • Public reporting • Board leadership • Management succession planning • Compensation of management • Asset Managers' role in Corporate Governance	
	Principle 3: Boards should be responsive to shareholders and be proactive in order to understand their perspectives
	Principle 4: Board should have a strong, independent leadership structure
	Principle 5: Boards should adopt structures that enhance their effectiveness
	Principle 6: Boards should develop management incentive structures that are aligned with the long term structure of the company

Reporting on governance

Organisations are also required to report on their governance arrangements. The **Global Reporting Initiative standard 102**[32] includes a good section on governance, which requires that you report on:

✓ Governance structure
✓ Delegating authority
✓ Executive-level responsibility for economic, environmental, and social topics
✓ Consulting stakeholders on economic, environmental, and social topics
✓ Composition of the highest governance body and its committees
✓ Chair of the highest governance body
✓ Nominating and selecting the highest governance body
✓ Conflicts of interest
✓ Role of highest governance body in setting purpose, values, and strategy
✓ Collective knowledge of highest governance body
✓ Evaluating the highest governance body's performance
✓ Identifying and managing economic, environmental, and social impacts
✓ Effectiveness of risk management processes
✓ Review of economic, environmental, and social topics
✓ Highest governance body's role in sustainability reporting
✓ Communicating critical concerns
✓ Nature and total number of critical concerns

---

[32] https://www.globalreporting.org/standards

> ✓ Remuneration policies
> ✓ Process for determining remuneration
> ✓ Stakeholders' involvement in remuneration
> ✓ Annual total compensation ratio
> ✓ Percentage increase in annual total compensation ratio

Warning signs:

The following are all indications that governance in your organisation could be strengthened:

- **Lack of independence** of Trustees – where the CEO is also the Chairman (it can happen but needs to be carefully managed), where several of the Trustees have come from executive roles within the organisation, or where they have other vested interests that could compromise their independence.

- **Lack of diversity** – an over-concentration of one skill or set of backgrounds. This can happen with NEDs appointing colleagues and friends to boards. Compounded if everyone seems to be agreeing all the time at the Board – a phenomenon known as "groupthink".

- An **overly static** Board with long tenure and no changes. Lack of churn allows people to get too settled in their roles. It is important to have a fresh perspective.

- **Dominance** – one or more people playing an overly dominant role on the Board. The "dominant, bullying and manipulative Chairperson / CEO" has been responsible for many well-publicised corporate failures.

- **Apathy** – The presence of significant control issues, that don't improve over time. The Board being tolerant when progress is constantly reported "Amber": "We know we have issues, but we're working on them. We'll see how we do next quarter."

- **Roles and responsibilities not clear** / boundaries not clear. NEDs unsure if it's their place to intervene.
- Board meetings which **do not engage** the participants.

The perils of boring committee meetings.

Audit Committee meetings, for example, will rarely compete with a Hollywood blockbuster for entertainment value. On the other hand, if meetings have become dull page-turner events, something is wrong. Audit Committee meetings are a forum for topical discussions of the strategic and operational risks facing the organisation. The content discussed should be relevant and timely, and should be presented in plain English so as to empower and engage every committee member.

A good Audit Committee should also make the executives slightly squirm in their seats by reinforcing the key issues in their heads and providing fresh impetus to resolve the issues raised by the next quarter – or risk facing a roasting by their committee members. I never appreciated the role of an Audit Committee as much as when they were straightening out our vision, cutting through the noise, landing a real issue with me, and sending me out with fresh urgency to get an issue remediated.

- **Too much information** being presented. It's hard to see the substantive topics if they are buried under too much information. If an agenda is weighted towards presentation, with little or no time for discussion, the organisation isn't getting the most out of its NEDs.

- A **culture** where substantive probing / questioning is discouraged or closed down. You don't want a governance meeting which is merely "theatre" or a well-rehearsed presentation intended to make everything appear to be in order and on track.

CASE STUDY: The collapse of Kids Company[33]

Kids Company, a high profile UK charity, collapsed in August 2015. This had a damaging impact on the vulnerable beneficiaries it sought to help, as well as on its staff, trustees, and politicians, including the Prime Minister who had supported it. It sent reverberations throughout the not-for-profit sector. The Public Administration and Constitutional Affairs Committee ("PACAC") conducted an investigation into what led to the collapse. The key findings included:

- "Kids Company relied on a hand-to-mouth existence and by refusing to prioritise the building of any significant reserves, the trustees failed to exercise their duty of care towards the charity's clients, employees and donors. (Paragraph 221).
- Kids Company did not have a clear plan to manage cash flow ups and downs but relied on fundraisers and government to make up shortfalls (paragraph 25).

---

[33] "Charities Alert: The collapse of Kids Company: Lessons to be learned", *Deloitte*

- Kids Company over-inflated figures relating to its caseload. Trustees were either ignorant of this exaggeration or simply accepted it, because it helped to promote the charity's fundraising (paragraph 35).
- Kids Company did not respond to Ofsted concerns (paragraph 40).
- PACAC found it "difficult to see on what basis Kids Company's trustees satisfied themselves of the appropriateness of support given to clients, and the value for money offered by the charity's high resource model...This approach left the trustees unable to defend the reputation of Kids Company which is a prime obligation of the good governance and leadership of any organisation" (paragraph 47).
- The handling of an allegation of a very serious failure in safeguarding was inadequate and irresponsible (paragraph 59).
- There was a lack of relevant trustee expertise in the field of youth services and psychotherapy (paragraph 68).
- There was a clear link between the failure to correct serious weaknesses in the organisation, and the failure to refresh its leadership (paragraph 68).
- No changes were made in response to management letters from auditors and repeated warnings about the charity's low levels of reserves and Kids Company's extensive use of contracted and self-employed workers despite concerns being raised with trustees (paragraph 74).

- There should be particular caution towards boards in which trustees have held their positions for more than two terms, and towards boards where no individuals have experience in the charity's particular area of delivery (paragraph 162)".

The shockwaves of this extreme example of inadequate governance are still being felt, with the possibility of the Trustees being disqualified for life from operating on future Boards[34].

Good to great

Maintaining good governance is an achievement in itself, and it's hard to speak in general terms about "great" governance. However, there is always scope to achieve greater synergy between the Executive and Non-Executive functions. When a diverse group of NEDs brings all its knowledge to bear on your organisation's challenges, challenging but supporting you, the resulting chemistry can be a genuine source of competitive advantage. You emerge from a really good Board meeting exhausted but stimulated, with a clearer sense of priority and an insight or two on how to break through the most stubborn issues that are holding the organisation back. You also see great governance and the true qualities of people when an organisation is going through a difficult period. Who shows up – and how they show up – tells you everything you need to know about the character of your Trustees.

---

[34] http://news.sky.com/story/government-moves-to-ban-kids-company-directors-over-2015-collapse-10849147

Current hot topics

Governance failures and the role of Boards. Once upon a time, becoming a Non-Executive Director of a business or a charity was a prestigious and lucrative opportunity. You got paid (in the private sector at least) to read some papers, to show up four times a year to meetings where you asked a few intelligent questions, networked with your impressive peers, then disappeared until the next quarter. Recent governance failures in both the private and charitable sectors have placed a spotlight on Boards like never before. Non-Executives typically value their reputations far more than the sums they get paid as NEDs. Right now, given the reputational damage that some NEDs have suffered, some might question whether it's worth the risk to take on these positions. Organisations can find it difficult to attract the non-executive talent they need, and particularly to attract candidates from diverse backgrounds. It's a competitive market. To respond to this, an organisation must accentuate the positives of the role (reputation, influence, networking opportunities, a sense of purpose) and minimise the negatives (through strong risk management and robust reporting), in order to remain attractive to the Non-Executive Director talent base.

Checklist of policies

- Memorandum and Articles of Association
- Terms of Reference of the Board and all committees
- Delegation of Authority (see also Legal chapter)

Ten questions to ask about governance

1. What is the composition of the Board – who are they, how long have they been there, what are their backgrounds and skills?

2. How often do they meet and what topics have they discussed over the past 1-2 years?

3. How are the appointments to the Board made? How long are appointments for? What is the schedule of re-appointment?

4. Does the Board self-assess its effectiveness?

5. How is the remuneration of the senior executives set?

6. Who oversees the finances of the organisation? Is there a Finance Committee?

7. Where do Internal Audit and External Audit report? What independent line of escalation can they pursue if they have concerns?

8. When and how are the risks of the organisation discussed and understood?

9. Are there dominant personalities on the Board?

10. Do the Board members have particular areas of expertise that could be harnessed for the good of the organisation?

Case study: The Co-Operative Bank[35]

Co-Op Bank was a division of the Co-Op Group. In 2014, it failed a stress test and revealed that it required £1.5 billion funding following the takeover of another building society. Sir Christopher Kelly performed a review of the events leading to the capital shortfall at the Co-Operative bank. The report was published on 31 April 2014. It found that the key weakness was governance, saying that 'the existing governance structure has badly let down the Co-Operative group's members.' It also found significant failures on the part of the Board. In total, the report identified 15 lessons to be learnt from the problems at the Co-operative bank. The headlines were:

- The Group board failed to exercise effective oversight of the Bank, with the board's size and lack of commercial and banking expertise limiting how it performed its responsibilities. Kelly also said 'one of the most surprising features of this whole episode is that the Board seemed unaware of its limitations.'
- The Board was 'heavily reliant' on the Executive team when it came to commercial matters, suggesting in the face of a 'strong willed chief executive' the board was 'too weak to hold him adequately to account.'

The impact of that failure still reverberates today. In April 2017, the Co-Op announced[36] it would suffer a further £140 million loss in writing off its stake in the bank.

---

[35] "Governance at the Co-op." Leadership Foundation for Higher Education. Accessed June 4, 2017. https://www.lfhe.ac.uk/en/governance-new/resource-bank/previous-news-alerts/governance-at-the-coop.cfm.

Further reading

https://www.frc.org.uk/Our-Work/Publications/Corporate-Governance/UK-Corporate-Governance-Code-April-2016.pdf

https://www.gov.uk/government/uploads/system/uploads/attachment_data/file/589944/CC26.pdf

Foley, S.: "The battle of the US corporate governance codes." *Financial Times*, February 5, 2017

http://www.ey.com/Publication/vwLUAssets/EY-ICSA-the-nomination-committee-coming-out-of-the-shadows/$FILE/EY-ICSA-the-nomination-committee-coming-out-of-the-shadows.pdf

http://www.governancecode.org/wp-content/uploads/2012/06/Code-of-Governance-Full1.pdf

---

[36] Butler, Sarah. "Co-operative Group to write off the value of its stake in Co-op bank." *The Guardian*, 3 Apr. 2017. Web. 4 June 2017. <https://www.theguardian.com/business/2017/apr/03/co-operative-group-to-write-off-the-value-of-its-stake-in-co-op-bank>.

11. LEGAL

Note: I'm not a lawyer. The below is not intended to be a complete or accurate list of current legal issues. This is a non-lawyer's assessment of some of the key moving parts in the legal sector. Talk to your General Counsel and / or legal advisors for more information.

What this department does

The in-house Legal department, headed by the General Counsel ("GC"), manages the legal affairs of the organisation, from incorporation through managing litigation, to drafting and maintaining contracts.

Different leaders have very different attitudes to the Legal department. In one case I observed, the CEO treated their GC as their *consigliere*, and consulted them on every decision. In another case, the Legal team was treated in a much more transactional way, only called in to advise on contracts or litigation.

Not surprisingly, most in-house GCs would appreciate being closer to the leadership of their organisation[37]. Data from the CEB 2013 Legal Productivity and Efficiency Diagnostic Survey showed that 58% of General Counsel surveyed said that their *actual* legal role was as service provider; however, 85% said their *ideal* legal role would be one of strategic partner.

---

[37] http://legalexecutiveinstitute.com/5740-2/

In smaller organisations particularly, in-house Counsel have to be the general practitioners of the organisation – they must have skills across a range of broad disciplines. One minute they might be advising the CEO on a litigious matter, the next they are reviewing a contract, the next they are negotiating the best rates from an external law firm. Lawyers who are technically excellent as well as fungible and adaptable are hard to come by and extremely valuable.

In larger firms, greater specialisation becomes possible. You will have lawyers who deal in nothing but commercial contracts, nothing but competition law, nothing but litigation. Asking one of them about a topic outside of their chosen field is akin to asking a brain surgeon about your heart problem – you may get a blank stare. The size, cost and specialisation of your legal team will be in direct proportion to the industry you are in, the size of the organisation, how litigious an environment it is and how rigorously it is regulated. In areas where there are risks around public or employee safety, such as pharmaceuticals or the extractive industries, you will need a particularly strong bench of legal talent.

Roles and responsibilities

Memorandum & Articles of Association – Legal is responsible for the drafting, filing and holding in custody the incorporation documents of the organisation.

Delegation of Authority – Usually done by the General Counsel, or the CFO. This document defines who is allowed to make commitments on behalf of the organisation, and the limits on their powers.

Directors and Officers ("D&O") liability insurance. Holding insurance to protect the Directors of the organisation against certain actions brought against them in the discharging of their responsibilities.

Understanding and advising on the **legal context** within which the organisation operates, including legislation and case law.

Legal specialisms

- **Commercial contracts.** Negotiating, drafting and holding custody of the major contracts the organisation has with its counterparties.
- **Intellectual Property rights and protection.** Protection of intellectual or creative work from within the organisation. Monitoring and protecting the brands, patents and trademarks of the organisation, as well as ensuring that employees don't breach the IP rights of others.
- **Competition law / antitrust.** Ensuring the organisation does not fall foul of competition law, and responding if it is a victim of anti-competitive practice.
- **Employee Relations** (may sit in HR). Advising and interpreting on legislation and case law relating to industrial relations.
- **Litigation.** Responding to claims against the organisation and initiating claims on behalf of the organisation.

> - **Taxation law.** Interpreting and applying tax law in all the jurisdictions in which the organisation operates.

Legal support. There may also be administrative staff supporting the Legal team in areas such as technology and law firm panel management.

Overlaps

The Legal team is empowered to work with all parts of the organisation. Particular areas of interaction for Legal include:

- With **Supply Chain Management** for contract negotiation.
- With the **Public Relations team**, pertaining to reputation, libel, media mentions and intellectual property rights and protection.
- With **Compliance** in applying laws and sector-specific regulation to the organisation.

Relationships to watch.

The relationship with the CEO is an important bellwether for how Legal is perceived by the rest of the organisation.

Another important relationship is with Sales and Marketing. When a key contract with a new client is about to be signed, the temptation is for the Sales teams to sign it, almost at all costs. This needs to be tempered by the view of the Legal team. Your input here as referee is important.

In-house vs. outsourced

A key consideration in your evaluation of the Legal department is how much work is done in-house vs. outsourced to legal firms, and how the department arrived at this balance. There is no one right formula, but there are advantages to each.

In house counsel	Outsourced
✓ Deep knowledge of the organisation	✓ Ultimate in flexibility
✓ Always available	✓ Get best in class specialism on the topic
✓ Less expensive	✓ Can be conflicts of interest / can't always get the firm you want
✓ Training up the next generation / succession	✓ Reassuring to the Executive and Board that you have an authoritative source
✓ Corporate knowledge stays in the organisation	✓ Independence / lack of internal bias

Any strength overplayed becomes a weakness, and the *overuse* of one or another can have the following undesired effects:

In house counsel	Outsourced
✗ Lack of fresh thinking	✗ Highly expensive model
✗ In-house teams may not be expert in all fields	✗ Corporate knowledge is lost
	✗ Confidence of internal team is damaged

Industry frameworks

In the UK, the main acts of legislation are the UK Companies Act 2006 and the Insolvency Act 1986. In the US, key pieces of legislation include:

- Securities Act 1933
- Securities & Exchange Act 1934
- Sarbanes-Oxley Act 2002
- Dodd-Frank Act 2010
- Model Business Corporation Act
- State law

On top of this, there are EU Directives and relevant case law in relevant jurisdictions.

Duties of a Director under UK Company law

As COO, you may well be deemed a Director of your organisation. If so, and you are in the UK, you have a number of legal duties under the Companies Act 2006[38]. These are:

- A duty to act in accordance with the powers set out in the company's articles;
- A duty to promote the success of the company for the benefit of its members;
- A duty to exercise independent judgment;
- A duty to exercise reasonable care, skill and diligence;
- A duty to avoid conflicts of interest;
- A duty not to accept benefits from third parties; and
- A duty to declare to the company's other Directors any interest a Director has in a proposed transaction or arrangement with the company.

Familiarise yourself with these duties, and seek advice if you are unsure of what any of them mean to you.

Best practice for law firm panel management

Many organisations have a "panel" of external law firms that they outsource work to. Whatever the size and sophistication of your law panel, it's important that the organisation agrees and sets expectations for what the partner firms are going to provide.

Law firm panels should be reviewed periodically. When you review the panel (every 2-3 years at a minimum), you should have

---

[38] http://www.legislation.gov.uk/ukpga/2006/46/part/10/chapter/2

set criteria against which to assess the firms – and take decisions about whom to add, keep or remove.

The four criteria that Barclays[39] uses to assess its law firm panel

1. Legal advice

- Excellent technical expertise in relevant legal areas, including from other firms as appropriate.
- Provide lawyers who are commercial, and understand our position as a regulated institution.
- Ensure effective quality control across all matters.
- Advice incorporates the firm's collective experience in the industry or area of law.
- Bring a strategic approach to all legal matters.
- Thought leadership

2. Always deliver the collective experience of the firm.

- Look beyond the particular matter to consider policy consequences and long-term trends.
- Provide advice and guidance on innovation in the profession.
- Collaboration and teamwork

3. Operate as an extension of our own in-house team.

- Work collaboratively with other Barclays firms.
- Develop understanding of Barclays' businesses and objectives.

---

[39] http://www.inhouselawyer.co.uk/index.php/mag-feature/on-the-menu/

- Harness the value of lawyers working across multiple areas by sharing insight from their experiences with Barclays.

4. Value for money
- Understand the commercial drivers of legal costs.
- Offer ideas for increasing cost-effectiveness of legal services.
- Provide accurate cost estimates and timely notice if changes are to be considered.
- Avoid a 'win at all costs' mentality by talking to Barclays about cost-value trade-offs.
- Provide professionals who are trained in industry standards.

Applying project management principles to legal work

I have worked in Project Management and also supported a large Legal team, and I believe that lawyers can benefit greatly from applying core project management principles to legal work, saving considerable uncertainty and cost along the way.

Define – Develop – Test – Implement

Some of the key principles of project management have clear applicability for conducting legal work. Project Management theory states that:

- You break the work into manageable pieces, with clear stage gates before you start incurring time and cost on the next stage.

- You don't progress to the next stage of a project until you have finished the previous stage. So, for example, you don't proceed into detailed design until you have agreed terms of reference and sponsorship for a piece of work.
- You don't commence detailed work until the requirements have been agreed.

I have seen Legal teams take on large, complex pieces of work shunning any kind of visible structure, believing the subject matter to be too complicated. Good lawyers don't rush ahead. Instead, they take their time to structure the work, to explain it to their teams and only then to progress through the logical steps.

Categorising and costing legal work

The other benefit of applying project management principles is that different types of work can be charged in a transparent way back to the user. Lawyers instinctively shy away from this, a little insulted that their work can be offered as a commoditised service. However, knowing what an hour of an experienced partner-level resource vs. a paralegal costs enables better decision-making. Otherwise, people will go to their tried and trusted top-tier partner for every bit of advice, thinking "Why not get the best every time?" An understanding of the costs will demonstrate why this is not a good strategy.

Warning signs

Be alert to the following signs that your Legal department might need support.

A Legal team that is perceived as weak or irrelevant. As with Risk teams, an organisation only gets as good a Legal team as it deserves. If it has been under-funded, overlooked in favour of external counsel, or had its advice ignored, you can expect it to be demoralised and lacking in talent. Regardless of the degree to which you utilise external counsel, you need a strong internal Legal team, that knows its responsibilities and boundaries, and has confidence that, when it gives advice, its leadership will listen. This doesn't mean that leadership will always follow legal advice to the letter – it is, after all, still advice – but you and your CEO should always have a good, documented reason for why you chose not to follow their advice, and can justify it after the fact.

Lack of systems. In spite of the perception that many have of Legal being a world of quills and paper, progressive Legal departments are harnessing technical capability just as much as any other area. Systems can perform contract generation (e.g. in creating standard ISDAs for financial services firms), catalogue legal commitments and perform discovery in litigation. Some Legal departments are in the early stages of using data and analytics for decision support. Your General Counsel should be aware of the potential applications of technology and willing to embrace them.

Inability to catalogue or source existing contracts on request. Who has responsibility for custody of legal documents? In some organisations, it is the Legal team. In others, it is the business area that has signed the contract. I have frequently seen the Legal team favour the latter – however, I favour the former. Disseminating legal contracts and expecting different teams to have their own systems for cataloguing contracts is likely to lead to lost contracts, files not well-indexed, and is a nightmare if, as in the case of the banks, you are asked to extract every single investment or PPI contract you ever entered into. Management of original contracts and contemporaneous written records is easy to do correctly, but is catastrophic when done badly or not at all.

Excessive spending on external counsel, without good reason. As shown above, there are definite advantages to having a strong, engaged, third party legal panel to use in times of need. However, left unchecked, this can become a very expensive crutch, hollowing out your Legal team, letting your corporate knowledge float out the door and creating a dependency that is hard to wean the organisation off. Equally, a completely closed approach, where specialist legal firms are never referred to, could mean that the organisation doesn't have access to the most up to date thinking.

Long, ongoing contracts with law firms with unspecified work. Law firms will happily keep their chargeable hours going against unspecified ongoing work. The Legal team should exercise sound quality control over legal instructions, to ensure the work is tightly defined, with timelines and clear deliverables. This can be difficult, say, at the outset of litigation, when not enough is known about the case. In this event, the work should be broken down, defining the first phase and having a clear decision gate before moving to the next. The law firm panel management team can help in determining the optimal pricing method (fixed price or "per hour") is best in each case.

A false sense of confidence. If your in-house lawyer tells you with confidence that "we will definitely win this case", challenge and probe. If a case goes to court, there are so many moving parts that the outcome can never be certain. This is known as "litigation risk".

Good to great

World-class Legal teams are asking themselves the following questions:

Whether **Technology** can be used to improve or automate key processes, such as the generation and cataloguing of contracts. Document editing and review solutions are making it easier than ever to outsource drafting, process mark-ups and securely sign binding contracts, without paper. Technology solutions can also identify whether and where a contract has been edited. This can save a lot of money, particularly with high-volume repetitive contracts, such as ISDAs in financial services. Expect **Blockchain** to contribute more in this area, where indelible records will make contract signing, identity verification and non-repudiation even more secure.

Innovative approaches to sourcing legal work. Not all legal work needs to be done by qualified lawyers. Good lawyers are aware of the high and lower-value aspects of their work, and where they can put their scarce time to the best use. Lower-end repetitive tasks can be automated, outsourced and / or offshored to low cost paralegals around the world. Countries with common law jurisdictions, where there is a long-established rule of law and high quality educational institutions, provide significant opportunities for legal work to be offshored at much lower cost.

Current hot topics

General Data Protection Legislation **("GDPR")**. As mentioned in the Risk chapter, the GDPR was agreed in April 2016 and comes into effect on May 2018. It proposes sweeping changes in the approach to personal data, and raises the sanctions for non-compliance to much greater heights.

Brexit. What it will mean for "passporting" and enforceability of contracts as well as immigration rules. EU passporting allows financial services organisations that are authorised in any one EU or EEA state to trade freely in any other with minimal additional authorisation – this may change post Brexit.

Market Abuse Regulation ("MAR"). The revised MAR came into force in July 2016 and has put increased specificity around the obligations of organisations to monitor suspicious transactions, market soundings and wall-crossings.

Dividends / creditors – responsibilities of Directors. The issue of torrid investor dividends has weighed large in recent years. Directors face an important set of responsibilities in weighing up dividends against the other obligations of the organisation. A recent case in the UK High Court demonstrated that, before setting dividends, Directors must carefully evaluate all contingent and prospective liabilities, in terms of both size and likelihood, to ensure creditors' interests are not damaged, or risk personal liability and criminal sanctions.

Human rights and modern slavery. The arrival of the Modern Slavery Act in the UK in 2015 has catapulted this issue to the forefront. Legal liabilities for getting this wrong are severe. The reputational risk of uncovering modern slavery in your supply chain is considerable. Your organisation has to have robust assessment processes all along its supply chain, and all employees need to be sensitised to the issues. From a legal perspective, expect to see explicit covenants or warranties requiring compliance with human rights to become a standard feature in contracts.

Blockchain – Used to authenticate contracts and provide non-repudiation.

Automation of decision-making, advice and contract generation. IBM now has an artificial intelligence prototype, called Watson, which it claims is providing better advice than some lawyers!

Big data / tools for discovery. In the past, junior paralegals would spend hours wading through countless pages of emails or contracts looking for a particular name or word reference. Now, documents and email servers can be searched at a rate of millions of words per minute. Even paper contracts can be reliably scanned.

Personal liability / clawback for directors / designated persons. In financial services, in response to the market crash of 2008, regulators are putting ever-increasing clawback provisions on remuneration and incentives, sometimes up to seven years after the remuneration is awarded.

Value for money including time recording. This is a contentious issues for lawyers! In law firms, lawyers have to account and bill for their time, sometimes in six-minute increments. This can feel stressful and intrusive, even with some of the automated solutions out there, which infer from what is active on the lawyer's computer screen which client you are working for. Many in-house lawyers cite time reporting as a reason to move out of law firms and into corporate organisations. However, there are substantial benefits to having time recording in place in Legal departments. These must be weighed against the pain of collecting the data.

Transparency. In most cases, the legal budget is held in the Legal department, with little cross-charging to the teams that consume Legal time. This can create a dysfunctional lack of moral hazard. If people don't realise the cost of what they're asking of their Legal teams, they will not feel incentivised to (a) keep out of situations where they need lawyers (b) be organised and structured when they approach their Legal teams for assistance, or (c) find better value at a lower cost. If you implement a method of costing and cross-charging Legal work back to departments, this can quickly raise their awareness of the cost implications.

Checklist of policies

- Law firm panel management – who the organisation refers work to, tendering processes, authorisation limits, etc.
- Competition law policy.
- Intellectual Property policy.
- Procedures in case of regulatory enquiry / investigation.

- Use of third party contracts policy.
- When employees should seek legal guidance.

Ten questions to ask your General Counsel

1. Where is the organisation registered and domiciled? Who are the registered Directors?
2. What is the legal structure of the organisation and its subsidiaries? Where is control / decision making taking place?
3. What are the delegation of authority arrangements? Who exactly is authorised to sign on behalf of the organisation?
4. What decisions are the CEO / COO and other executives empowered to make and when do they need to escalate to the Board?
5. What is the organisation empowered to do / not to do in its Memorandum and Articles of Association?
6. What major litigation is currently underway?
7. Does the organisation use external legal firms? Does it have a panel? How are instruction decisions made?
8. Who are our key suppliers and when were agreements last negotiated?
9. What insurance protection is in place to protect the Directors?
10. How is customer / client data confidentiality maintained and is the organisation ready for GDPR?

Further reading

www.inhouselawyer.co.uk – For topical updates from M&A to arbitration

12. COMPLIANCE

What this department does

The objective of Compliance is to ensure that the organisation has designed, implemented and is operating appropriate systems of control to manage regulatory risk. In addition, Compliance supports all areas of the organisation in their duties to comply with the law, industry regulation and internal procedures.

Compliance is a major growth area. In financial services, Compliance exploded following the credit crisis of 2008. In the mining & extractives sector, project failures and fatalities have led Boards and shareholders to demand stronger Compliance departments; in pharmaceuticals, product safety and suitability must be constantly assured and demonstrated.

Like Risk and Legal, Compliance is a *second line of defence* function (see Risk chapter for a definition of this). Every staff member has a role to play in upholding the standards of the organisation and it is important you set that tone when communicating with staff.

In smaller organisations, Compliance can be part of the Legal or Risk departments. In highly regulated industries, such as banking and pharmaceuticals, organisations have standalone, highly specialised departments.

> **Definition of regulation**
>
> A set of binding rules issued by a private or public body with the necessary authority to supervise compliance with them, and to apply sanctions in response to violation of them.

The purpose of regulation, regardless of the sector, is to:

- Protect the public and maintain public confidence
- Ensure efficient, fair and transparent markets
- Reduce risk across the sector
- Prevent and detect criminal activity

Whatever sector you work in, you are likely to have regulation covering some or all of the following:

- Product or service specifications
- How you market and advertise your product
- How you assess suitability of your product or service for your customers
- How you contract with your customers
- The service you provide to your customers
- How you manage conflicts of interest
- How you perform due diligence up and down your value chain

The scope, size and cost of your Compliance department will be influenced by the sector you are in, the size and complexity of your organisation and the nature of your customer base (business to business or business to consumer, sophisticated clients vs. members of the public).

In short, Compliance is about protecting the reputation and integrity of your organisation. Get this wrong, and, not only will the organisation incur fines and face censure, your personal reputation will take a battering that can be hard to recover from.

Roles and responsibilities

1. **Risk identification, mapping and advisory.** Identifying new trends and regulations, and preparing the organisation to meet them.

2. **Design of controls** to mitigate or prevent those risks from materialising.

3. **Rule setting.** Setting the internal boundaries for acceptable and unacceptable behaviour, with reference to industry practice.

4. **Reviewing, monitoring and reporting** on the effectiveness of the control environment.

5. **Response.** Dealing with the impact of compliance issues when they occur.

6. **Interpretation of rules and regulations**, and ongoing business advisory and partnering

7. **Regulatory relations.** Your Compliance staff will typically be the ones to own the relationship with your regulators. They will be the first point of contact - inbound if the regulator has a concern, outbound if the organisation has something to report.

8. **Filing / reporting.** Mandatory reporting, either on a periodic basis or in response to an incident.

9. **Training.** Defining the mandatory training that all employees must take, together with what declarations they need to sign, such as a code of conduct.

10. **Policy setting.** Setting some of the core policies of the organisation, and ensuring that the overall policy framework is sound.

11. **Culture.** The Compliance department's tone and strength are key to setting the culture. What standards are expected? Zero accidents? Zero tolerance? Reasonable endeavours? Compliance plays a role in setting the red lines of an organisation – and you and the rest of the Executive team must demand that they are respected.

12. **Surveillance and detection.** In some sectors, such as financial services, Compliance will play a technical surveillance role, monitoring trades for market abuse, conflicts of interest etc.. This is a highly specialised, and expensive, area.

> **The golden rule of good regulatory relations - early warning and no surprises.** Regulators appreciate regular and early contact. They want to be told when an issue is simmering, before it boils over. The one sure way to antagonise your regulator is for them to find out you have a problem by reading it in the morning papers. It makes them look bad, it makes you look bad. Early warnings are always appreciated. Build rapport with your regulators, so when you do have a problem, they will be helpful, believing in your good faith. Relationships are everything here.

Overlaps

Expect to see strong relationships between Compliance, Legal and Risk, with each playing slightly different roles.

There will be overlaps with Operations for product and service specifications, and in demonstrating sound product testing.

Compliance may work with Facilities to oversee building safety and security regulations.

Finally, Compliance works with HR to design and oversee employee awareness programmes and training requirements.

Relationships to watch

As with Legal and Risk, the relationship of the CEO to Compliance is a strong indicator of culture. Does the CEO listen to the Head of Compliance? Does he / she act upon their advice? What tone is the CEO setting regarding Compliance? Have they themselves done their mandatory training? Do they observe the conflict of interest policy? These markers are enormously significant in how staff perceive the importance of Compliance in their day to day work. A red flag is a CEO whose attitude is to "get this through Compliance". You want a CEO who understands that Compliance is a strategic partner, and who has taken the time to understand the principles and the rationales of the relevant regulations.

The other key relationship is with the Sales teams. How well does the front office respect the principles set out by Compliance? What power does Compliance have to take action if the rules are broken? What is the history of enforcement? Do senior executives roll their eyes or change their tone when referring to Compliance?

Industry frameworks

Given the international and sector-specific nature of compliance regulation, any list that claims to cover the compliance regime in its entirety is going to be incomplete. Below are some authorities that are likely to affect most industries, as well as some of the key current topics facing each industry at time of writing. Your Compliance team should be able to furnish you with a more comprehensive list as it relates to your sector and organisation.

Most organisations have to adhere to regulation concerning Governance, Competition law, Risk Management and Data Protection. Key regulators / competent authorities applicable to most UK and US firms include:

- US Department of Justice
- The Office of Foreign Assets Control / US Department of the Treasury
- EU Commission
- EU Competition Authority
- British Standards Institute
- The Information Commissioner's Office

Sector	Current Compliance considerations
Financial services	<ul><li>Know your customer</li><li>Anti-money laundering</li><li>Sanctions and politically exposed persons</li><li>Transparency and taxation</li></ul>
Automotive, logistics and transportation	<ul><li>Passenger safety</li><li>Modern slavery</li></ul>
Consumer products and retail	<ul><li>Trade descriptions</li><li>Product safety</li><li>Fairness in advertising</li><li>Statutory rights</li><li>Product testing</li><li>Packaging</li></ul>
Government and public sector	<ul><li>Fundraising standards</li><li>Donor privacy</li><li>Ethical procurement</li><li>Conflicts of interest</li></ul>
Science & Health care	<ul><li>Ethical testing</li><li>Product suitability</li><li>Clinical standards</li><li>Marketing</li></ul>
Media and entertainment	<ul><li>Journalistic integrity</li><li>Intrusion vs. public right to know</li></ul>
Energy and extractives	<ul><li>Sustainability</li><li>Impact on local communities</li><li>Worker safety</li></ul>
Real estate, travel, hospitality & construction	<ul><li>Worker safety</li><li>Safe construction</li></ul>
Technology and telecommunications	<ul><li>Competition law</li><li>Consumer protection</li></ul>

Food producers and processors	• Safeguarding consumers • Improving public health • Transparency • Food safety and hygiene • Food chain
Utilities	• Safety standards • Measurement / estimation / safety • Consumer choice and flexibility
Industrial and engineering	• Safety standards
Service industries	• Professional indemnity insurance • Conflicts of interest

General characteristics of a strong Compliance regime

Over and above the regulation and regional differences, there is a general set of characteristics that any regulator (and therefore also you) will be on the lookout for, as indicators of strong Compliance.

- **Commitment from the top.** The Board, CEO, COO and Executive team should be setting the tone for compliance. Has the organisation hired a strong Head of Compliance? Is the Head of Compliance on the Executive Committee? If commitment from the top is not evident, then the relationship with the regulator will likely be fractious and ultimately unsuccessful.
- A **framework** for identifying, assessing and dealing with risks, including:
  - o Appropriate delegation of authority and roles & responsibilities assignment, including consideration of conflicts and segregation of duties

- o Strong process and system design
- o Alignment of incentives for staff to do the right thing
- o Clear setting of standards, including training and awareness
- o Preventive and detective controls
- o The ability to detect transgressions and act upon them
- o Appropriate disciplinary and reporting procedures
- **Adequate resourcing** of the Risk and Compliance side of the organisation, in terms of seniority, skills and numbers, appropriate to the size of the revenue-generating arm.
- An ongoing cycle of **review, improvement and learning.**

Organisational design considerations for Compliance

One key decision is where in the organisation to locate your Compliance team and whether to position them as a single team or distributed across the organisation. Both have benefits and pitfalls. A single, centralised team will benefit from scale, plus staff will enjoy reinforcement from working alongside like-minded professionals. On the other hand, they may struggle to infiltrate and understand the departments they are overseeing. If you embed Compliance staff within front office teams, this can result in better visibility of what's going on. Embedded Compliance staff can pick up a lot of useful information through their co-location with the teams. They can however run the risk of "going native", i.e. being overly influenced by the teams they are supposed to be overseeing.

You should also consider the composition of skills and experience of the Compliance team. Some of the best Compliance professionals are former front-line staff. Poachers turned gamekeepers know better than anyone else where the skeletons are buried, and what tricks people are likely to play. Having a few of these in your team can balance out the regulation-heavy focus with some real applied practice.

Warning signs

Watch out for the following:

An **acrimonious relationship** with the regulator. This is never a good thing. Beware the organisation that thinks it's smarter than the regulator. This complacency will eventually catch up with them.

A history of **fines** and **sanctions**, compounded with a lack of internal remorse and willingness to learn.

A regulator who is perceived as weak or stand-offish. This might not appear to be problematic in the short term, but over time, will allow problems to build up and boil over in the sector.

A Compliance team that appears to be **going through the motions**. Checking all the boxes, keeping the regulator happy, but not engaging in the "guts" of what the organisation is doing. Also, a Compliance team that's overly generalist, without the requisite in-depth knowledge of the products, services and processes will suffer from a lack of respect and engagement, resulting in issues being missed.

Good to great

A highly compliance-focused culture can contain some or all of the following characteristics.

A **culture of compliance** throughout the organisation. Where it's not seen as the role of the Compliance team, but of everyone, to do things in the right way.

A high degree of **identification with the customer** / end beneficiary. In financial services, this could manifest as people asking "Would I want to sell this product to my Dad / sister / friend?"

Compliance viewed as key **partners** – Compliance professionals being involved early, in the design phases of new products or services, when the right features can be built into the product from the get go.

Compliance professionals who are **not overly risk averse**, who really understand the environment and feel empowered to say "Yes, we can do this, as long as..." as well as "No". On balance, the number of times a Compliance function will be saying "No" should be small. If the Compliance function and the business are working well together, understanding the regulations within their industry, real confrontations should be few and far between.

High quality, relevant and realistic, multi-channel compliance **training**. Updated regularly, the right length, entertaining, high quality and not insulting the intelligence of staff.

Embedded compliance and monitoring. Where monitoring and surveillance are built in as part of organisational systems. This makes checking a seamless, real time, frictionless and invisible exercise.

Current hot topics

Governance. See chapter on Governance. This remains very much a hot topic, given corporate failures and the ongoing malaise following the 2008 financial crash.

Whistleblowing. A key aspect of any compliance regime is the existence of an appropriate, confidential, whistleblowing facility for staff to use where they see the wrong behaviours in existence. For whistleblowing to be credible, staff must believe they will be protected if they raise a concern in good faith and trust that their concern will be followed up on – organisations must prove this is the case.

Checklist of policies

- Code of conduct / employee handbook
- Mandatory training policy
- Conflicts of interest
- Anti-bribery and corruption policy
- Public / regulatory policy
- Anti-money laundering policy
- Whistleblowing policy
- Complaints policy
- Data protection policy
- Privacy policy – for employees and customers

Ten questions to ask

Ten questions to ask of Compliance

1. What regulation is the organisation subject to?
2. Has there been a regulatory audit / review in recent years? Are there any planned?
3. How often does the organisation communicate with its regulators and in what circumstances? How many times in the past year?
4. How would Compliance describe the relationship with the regulator?
5. What regulatory incidents have taken place in the past 24 months? Are there any open investigations?
6. What regulatory difficulties have competitors faced?
7. Is there a Compliance manual or code of conduct? Do employees sign up to it?
8. What mandatory training courses are employees required to undertake? What is the rate of uptake? What happens if staff don't complete the training?
9. How is customer / client data confidentiality maintained?
10. What support does the compliance team get from the rest of the organisation? Who are the most challenging internal stakeholders? What happens when a Compliance rule is breached?

Further reading

http://www.ethic-intelligence.com/wp-content/uploads/2014-SAI-Global-Program-Assessment-Maturity-Curve.pdf

https://www2.deloitte.com/content/dam/Deloitte/us/Documents/human-capital/us-cons-deloitte-regulatory-learning.pdf

13. Supply Chain Management

What this department does

Also called "Procurement", the Supply Chain Management ("SCM") department manages the planning, procuring, leasing, buying, storing and delivering goods and services – including materials, parts, supplies, services, equipment, fixtures and IT. Its remit ranges from setting strategy and policy to managing conflicts of interest, from anticipating needs to positioning supplies in the right place at the right time, from managing storage and wastage to dealing with fraud and ensuring your supply chain is ethical. This is a crucial department. If you neglect it, criminal and civil sanctions can result. Get to know your Head of SCM early on.

In certain industry sectors, such as pharmaceuticals or aerospace, SCM assumes an even greater level of sophistication, where item-level traceability is required, for quality and recall issues. It's expensive, high volume and complex. If you're in one of these sectors, this may consume a lot of your time as COO.

Case study: SCM in humanitarian organisations

In humanitarian organisations, the potential implications of SCM failures go way beyond waste and cost. These organisations must properly secure their supply chains to avoid the risk that terrorist organisations can infiltrate and steal much-needed goods. They need sophisticated forecasting ability to ensure that supplies are in the right place when they

---

are needed. They need fit-for-purpose transportation and storage facilities, or much needed food and vaccines may perish and never reach the people they were intended for. There are few things more important in these organisations than excellent procurement and logistics. The problem is that best-in-class systems and processes cost money and are still, in the minds of many donors, considered an "overhead" cost.

We wouldn't expect a consumer goods company to operate without sophisticated systems. Humanitarian organisations which save millions of lives every year should be entitled to the same. The Bill & Melinda Gates Foundation has written a paper entitled "Mobilising the Supply Chain Community to Solve Global Challenges[40]", in which it issues a call to action for SCM organisations to help humanitarian organisations through shared value partnerships. It contends that the private sector SCM community does not have to be involved in these types of partnerships just out of the goodness of its heart; there are also commercial benefits. These shared-value engagements can open up new markets, provide innovative research and development opportunities, and serve to develop the next generation of SCM leaders.

Roles and responsibilities

- **Strategy**. Setting the SCM strategy, aligned with the overall corporate strategy, to outline what resources (systems, people and processes) are required by the organisation, to

---

[40]   http://www.manufacturing-today-europe.com/2017/01/11/key-to-solving-world-issues/

procure and distribute the organisation's products and services.

- **Scheduling / forecasting.** Working with the Sales and Operations teams to forecast future demand levels, manage uncertainty and set expectations with suppliers for what volumes will be required over the coming period.
- **Supplier identification and assessment**, including ethical sourcing. This includes all aspects of managing suppliers - from assessing new suppliers, to dealing with non-performance or quality issues. It involves setting expectations for what the organisation wants from its suppliers, both quantitative (volumes, prices) and qualitative (quality, reliability, sustainability).
- **Tendering.** Supporting the organisation for its more substantial purchases, this involves researching the market, creating supplier long lists, designing and conducting the assessment process, defining the success criteria, evaluating suppliers and choosing the winning pitch.
- **Spot buying.** Putting in place adequate processes to ensure that the organisation gets the best value from its low-value purchases.
- **Commercial negotiation.** Securing the best possible deals, including consideration of volumes, prices, discounts, pricing models, penalty clauses and securing other value-added services.
- **Supplier management.** Managing the ongoing relationships with suppliers, to ensure they're delivering

maximum value and performing according to the standards and service levels that have been agreed upon.

- **Inventory management.** Calculating how much is needed and when, and how much stock to hold. The costs of inventory management include insurance, taxes, obsolescence and warehousing.

> **Total cost of inventory.** Acquisition costs often account for just 25-40% of the total cost for most products and services[41]. The balance comprises operating, training, maintenance, warehousing, environmental, quality and transportation costs.

- **Transportation and logistics.** Managing safe, reliable, appropriate and secure transportation of materials, using either in-house logistics staff or outsourced transportation specialists.
- **Environmental management.** Designing systems to prevent wastage, spillage and other incidents. Reporting them when they occur.
- **Security and risk management.** Ensuring that cargo is appropriately secured at every step along the value chain to prevent fraud and theft. Humanitarian organisations operating in certain conflict and fragile countries need to report any thefts to the authorities as potential terror events.

41

http://www.supplychainquarterly.com/topics/Procurement/scq201101bestpractices/

- **Reporting and monitoring** to Management on suppliers, costs, volumes and incidents.

Overlaps

The SCM department usually interacts with a wide range of stakeholders across the organisation:

- Finance for hedging contracts, currency and commodity exposures
- Operations, Sales and Marketing for forecasting and demand planning
- IT and Finance for significant non-production spend (e.g. IT systems, facilities)
- Legal for contract management
- Risk and Security teams for security, transport and storage issues
- Compliance when reporting significant issues to regulators

Relationships to watch

All significant spend activity should go through the SCM department. Facilities and IT spend should have the same level of rigour and oversight as procurement of stock in trade. This may not always be welcomed by teams who would prefer to follow their own process, and not take the time required to go through a formal tender. It can seem alluring to cut corners in SCM in order to get work moving quickly, but it's rarely the right thing to do. A proper procurement process can uncover options not previously thought of, identify more suitable vendors, and result in the negotiation of more preferential terms.

Industry frameworks

The most recognised standard, internationally and cross-sector, is the Global Standard for Procurement and Supply[42], by the Chartered Institute of Procurement & Supply (CIPS). More of a checklist of competencies than an industry standard, it sets out expectations for levels of competency for practitioners, across the following themes:

- Infrastructure
  - Position and influence
  - External environment
  - Technology
- Process
  - Spend management
  - Contracting
  - Sourcing
- Performance
  - Delivering outcomes
  - Metrics and measurement
- People development
  - Developing teams and individuals
  - Developing self and personal skills
  - Ethics

Another useful framework is the "Public Relations Procurement Toolkit"[43]. Intended for use by public relations professionals, it is

---

[42] https://www.cips.org/en-gb/careers/global-standard-for-procurement-and-supply/

[43] https://www.cipr.co.uk/content/policy-resources/toolkits-and-best-practice-guides/procurement-toolkit

capable of wider application. It contains 20 indicators of good practice in SCM:

1. "We build/maintain a well-managed roster of agencies and suppliers for individual categories of PR spend
2. We consider extending or scaling existing relationships before engaging with a new agency/supplier
3. We regularly review non-rostered agencies or suppliers to see where they could add value to the roster
4. We ensure that the selection of new agencies/suppliers is informed by a clear understanding of the need
5. We select agencies/suppliers via a comprehensive and structured process
6. All our PR suppliers of every type are fully and appropriately contracted
7. The complexity of the procurement steps we use varies so as to be appropriate to the size of the spend and/or the importance of the project
8. We consider carefully whether each activity should be carried out by a supplier which is local, regional or global
9. Whenever possible, we include a meaningful performance-related element within agency/supplier costs
10. We hold regular assessments of agency/supplier performance
11. We encourage strong, collaborative working relationships between different agencies/ suppliers
12. We achieve transparency and visibility in project cost estimates (e.g. via tools such as standard cost breakdown templates, rate cards)

13. We benchmark commercial proposals/costs with people with commensurate experience (including use of external, independent specialists)

14. We review proposed outputs to identify potential opportunities for re-scoping/re-specification (to achieve a more 'fit for purpose' result)

15. We require agencies/suppliers to flag and document any changes from cost estimates as activities/ projects progress

16. We convene regular budget management meetings - tracking committed and planned expenditure vs. budget

17. We ensure that post-activity evaluation includes discussions on how to improve cost efficiency for similar future activities

18. We capitalise on opportunities to consolidate spend (e.g. across markets or time periods)

19. We regularly assess value for money and return on investment for each category of spend

20. The nature of our procurement process in itself contributes to the creation of value for the organisation"

Warning signs for SCM

The following may indicate issues that require your early attention:

- **High levels of fraud and wastage.** A possible indicator of lack of oversight or security.

- **Perishable stock expiring**. An indication of either inadequate planning or inadequate storage and logistics arrangements.
- Significant, unhedged **price fluctuations** for commodity inputs. Your Head of SCM should have considered price hedging for commodity items and have a good rationale for the approach taken.
- Vendor agreements managed by **individual departments** (e.g. by the Heads of IT or Facilities), without support from SCM.
- **Lack of senior management recognition** for SCM. It's hard to enforce procurement standards if senior management are not respecting them.
- **Conflicts of interest** from Executive and Board members not being clearly highlighted. This exposes the organisation to cosy deals and lack of independence.
- **Fragmented / immature systems** covering SCM. This can be a highly complex area and needs appropriate system support along the entire purchase-to-pay life cycle.
- Frequent **disputes with suppliers**. An indication of possible problems with inbound logistics.
- **Slow payment** from customers. An indication of possible problems with outbound logistics or product quality, or insufficiently tight credit control.

Assessing your suppliers – the fundamentals

Your SCM department should have a set of criteria for supplier assessment. Some criteria will be specific to what you are procuring from them – product specifications, quality standards etc.. However, there are some fundamental criteria that all suppliers should be assessed against, including the following:

- **Financial strength and stability.** Sometimes neglected by organisations – Is the supplier financially strong enough? Will it be around next year, to continue to supply you?
- **Sanctions screening.** At a minimum, there are standard checks the organisation must perform to ensure you are not dealing with sanctioned or politically exposed persons. In addition, based on the ethical standing of the organisation, there may be further standards you wish to apply to organisations you procure from.
- **Cyber security standards.** Are the supplier's systems and safeguards up to scratch?
- **Human rights standards and modern slavery.** What does your supplier's own supply chain look like? How far back can they trace it? Are they (and you) sure that their supply chain is clean and ethical? Are they aware of and adhering to the latest provisions on modern slavery?
- **Value for money.** Are they providing the best commercial terms on that particular item or service? How can they help your organisation achieve the goals that you have set?
- **Historical performance.** Have they demonstrated the experience to deliver to the required scope and level of service required by your organisation?

SCM Organisational Design

You have a decision to make between having a single central SCM team vs. embedding the function within other departments. If you are seeking greater cost management and control, a centralised model can be preferable. In its paper "How to Create a Supply Chain Center of Excellence That Works" [44], Jonathan Whitaker outlines six success criteria for making a success of a Supply Chain Centre of Excellence:

1. "Start with a CoE readiness assessment" – find out whether you have the internal capability to support it.
2. "Ensure strong executive sponsorship and guidance" – the team will need support from a motivated and powerful executive in the organisation.
3. "Provide good analytical tools" – to empower the team to provide real insight.
4. "Bring core CoE team members together in one place" – the author contends that this boosts effectiveness.
5. "Develop a clear and meaningful career path for CoE team members" – to create succession and a strong pool of talent.
6. "Know when to call in reinforcements" – get the blend of internal resource and external specialism right.

---

[44] Whitaker, Jonathan. "How to create a supply chain center of excellence that works". Supply Chain Quarterly, 2016. Accessed June 10, 2017 http://www.supplychainquarterly.com/topics/Technology/20161021-how-to-create-a-supply-chain-center-of-excellence-that-works/

Good to great

So, you have established that SCM is essentially sound - appropriately resourced in terms of people and systems, with good adherence to procurement standards and on the right side of the law. Costs are reasonable, loss, fraud and wastage are minimised. If so, below are some of the ways you can take it to the next level.

From transactions to strategy. An evolved organisation understands that procurement is not just about a one-time price – it is more about value creation with its suppliers over the long term.

Source to pay systems – Implementing end-to-end systems covering all stages of the SCM life cycle, from sourcing to purchase order, to invoice, to payment. These systems track and match purchases every step of the way, with minimal human interaction and they integrate with finance and stock systems to provide meaningful decision support for management.

Automation. The use of solutions to automate payments and verification, thus shrinking lead times and releasing money that was previously trapped in the supply chain.

Artificial Intelligence / predictive modelling. The use of big data to predict what supplies will be needed, where and when, and sourcing those items before people even know they're needed.

Product life cycle management / demand and supply integration. These sophisticated techniques involve taking an end-to-end view of the organisation's value creation processes and optimising them by strengthening cross-organisational linkages, and simplifying and standardising the supply chain.[45]

Employee self-service. Putting power back in the hands of staff for small purchases, subject to appropriate constraints. This speeds up processes and removes red tape, leaving the SCM department to focus on the big-ticket items.

Great collaborative internal business relationships. Where the need for procurement expertise doesn't have to be drummed into people – they understand the benefit. Thoughtful SCM teams will engage with Sales & Marketing to understand what customers want. They will work with Operations to better understand the manufacturing process, and respond to these needs.

Mutually beneficial supplier relationships. Where fair prices are paid for quality goods and the organisations work together to continuously improve. Organisations may even collaborate to improve sustainability along the supply chain.

Value-add. Many not-for-profit organisations are extraordinarily brazen – and successful – in negotiating additional value added services from suppliers to make their scarce resources go even further. Whether it's additional training, use of office space or other pro bono services, these can often cost little to the supplier but be of enormous value to the purchaser. In addition, if they are helping a charity, the suppliers get bragging rights and their employees get to feel good. However, if these "perks" start to

---

[45] http://www.supplychainquarterly.com/topics/Manufacturing/20170303-using-supply-chain-enabled-plcm-to-boost-margin-growth/

overshadow the commercial terms and blur management thinking, an impartial SCM professional should step in.

Current hot topics

Retrenchment from globalisation in favour of local and ethical sourcing. This is exacerbated by a new sense of nationalism in the US and the UK.[46]

Efficiency / tightening of spend. In tough times, with Brexit bringing the possibility of price hikes in the UK, extracting efficiency and cost savings from the supply chain is on the mind of every senior executive. SCM has to be more innovative and agile than ever.

Better visibility. According to Aberdeen Group[47], the watchword of the moment is "visibility". Inbound supply chain visibility differentiates best-in-class SCM from the rest of the pack. This allows the really smart operators to see issues and take corrective action before problems occur, ensuring less disruption to inbound supply.

Modern slavery. In the light of recent legislation, all organisations are wisely re-examining how much they know about their supply chains and whether the risk of latent modern slavery is addressed.

---

[46] http://www.supplychainquarterly.com/columns/20161215-globalization-at-a-crossroad/
[47] "Supply chain visibility: know sooner, act now", Aberdeen Group

Sourcing as a competitive advantage. Making the sustainability and social good of your supply chain a differentiator – e.g. the Fairtrade brand.

Dealing with emerging markets challenges. Unstable markets, uncertain transportation lead times and fluctuating prices are just some of the issues for organisations sourcing from emerging markets.

Checklist of policies for procurement

- Local and ethical sourcing policy
- Tendering policy
- New supplier vetting policy
- Prevention of modern slavery policy

Ten questions to ask

1. Who has responsibility for Supply Chain Management?
2. Is the SCM department centralised or embedded within other departments?
3. Is there an SCM strategy? How does it link to the organisational strategy?
4. How much does the organisation procure every year? Across how many and what types of cost categories?
5. Who are the key suppliers to the organisation? Include suppliers of stock-in-trade, corporate goods and contractors / people. How competitive is the market?
6. Is there a preferred supplier list? What is the process for reviewing it? What is the tendering process?
7. What levels of fraud and wastage are being reported?

8. Does the organisation have an ethics policy relating to SCM? Is it up to date on modern slavery provisions, anti-terrorism, fraud?
9. What systems are used to plan, procure, store, distribute, track and pay for goods and services?
10. What are the challenges with warehousing and distribution?

Further reading

"Procurement toolkit." *CIPR (Chartered Institute of Public Relations)*

Rogers, D., Leuschner, R., Choi, T.Y.: "The Rise of FinTech in Supply Chains." *Harvard Business Review*

Chris G. Christopher, Jr. "Globalization at a crossroad?" *Supply Chain Quarterly*

Whitaker, J.. "How to create a supply chain center of excellence that *works*." *Supply Chain Quarterly*

Stank, T., Saunders, L., Burnette, M., Autry, C.. "Using supply chain-enabled PLCM to boost margin growth." *Supply Chain Quarterly*

"Supply Chain Visibility: Know Sooner, Act Now." *Aberdeen Group Report*

"Mobilising the Supply Chain Community to Solve Global Challenges: Engaging the Private Sector." *Bill & Melinda Gates Foundation*

14. Facilities Management

The Royal Institute of Chartered Surveyors defines strategic facilities management[48] as *"the effective management of place and space, integrating an organisation's support infrastructure to deliver services to staff and customers at best value whilst enhancing overall organisational performance."* I also like Dan Weiss's description[49]: *"It is about maximising how space contributes to productivity and to people's engagement with the organisation and its goals."*

The Facilities Management ("FM") team takes care of the day-to-day realities of your buildings and real estate. However, at their best, they are much more than this: customer-focused strategists, architects, accountants, builders, advocates, communicators and cross team facilitators. They're often the people who take the lead when a business interruption occurs. As COO you're responsible for the oversight of FM. Get to know this area well.

What this department does

Your facilities are where you house your people, your shops and your offices. They're also a key part of your organisational identity. Where they're located, what your reception looks like, what's on the walls, the colour scheme, how tidy it is, how you group people, what their workspaces look like, where you give

---

[48] https://www.fgould.com/uk-europe/articles/why-facilities-management-struggling-be-strategic/
[49] https://www.fgould.com/uk-europe/articles/why-facilities-management-struggling-be-strategic/

them to collaborate, where they eat, the water tap, the coffee, the ambient noise - every one of these details speaks volumes about your organisation. Good office space is a key retainer of talent. It can play a large role in motivating your people to do their best.

Facilities (along with people and technology costs) are likely to be some of the organisation's biggest expenditures, and owned premises the largest assets on your balance sheet.

Case study: Interplay of people and facilities

I inherited a project to refurbish our HQ building in its early stages. The building was stuck in the 1980s. Rising headcount meant we needed to optimise the use of the available space. The physical building refurbishment was a success – it was delivered on time and under budget, resulting in a brighter, more modern space with more capacity. However, the completion of the physical work was complicated. Moving staff from floor to floor was like a game of Tetris. Funds were limited, so we had to work hard to make them stretch. In addition to my taking on a project somebody else had scoped, the project manager changed halfway through, so continuity was an issue, and understanding why certain decisions had been made was a challenge.

We focused on just getting the project done and neglected the impact on people of having to move from fixed desks to hot desking. We didn't sufficiently manage and support the changes in their working habits. Line managers needed more guidance on what this meant for how they managed people.

Although I was a public and enthusiastic proponent of agile and flexible working arrangements, I know that not all staff got the same experience from their direct line managers. This resulted in dissonance between what was being said at the top and what was actually happening. The poor staff experience overshadowed the project. We circled back after the fact, created a change champions group, put in place training for line management and started a real conversation with our people about the experience they were having. We also made subsequent enhancements to the office space. I see now that, however difficult, allowing more time and awareness for the human element of the changes we were making would have made things smoother, and encouraged earlier adoption.

While other areas you oversee require real-time, day-to-day decision making, decisions regarding facilities can play out over years, if not decades. Long-term leases come with hefty break clauses; works take months or years to consult on, tender for, design and implement. This is what makes a strategy-led approach so important in this area. You must join your strategy and workforce planning with your facilities plans. Otherwise, you risk running out of space and having to respond with expensive short term fixes, or entering into substantial commitments just before you shed some of the workforce.

This is also an area in which neglect can lead to criminal charges. Fire safety, gas units, electricity tests, air conditioning hygiene, water quality, elevator maintenance, evacuation plans, health and safety foul ups – if you knowingly neglect these areas, penalties in the UK range from fines to imprisonment. Make sure your

Facilities manager is competent. You don't need gold-plated solutions in many cases, but you do need a well-serviced facility.

Roles and responsibilities

The following responsibilities are loosely taken from the British Institute of Facilities Management ("BIFM") professional standards framework and the Royal Institution of Chartered Surveyors ("RICS") strategic facilities management guidance. Facilities departments perform the following:

- Set the **facilities management strategy,** linked to the overall goals of the organisation.
- Establish **roles and responsibilities** and a **framework of policies and procedures** to achieve the FM strategy.
- Oversee and manage the **corporate estate portfolio,** making recommendations to management on how to optimise it.
- **Implement policies** in line with standards, e.g., building maintenance. Manage and review the maintenance agenda.
- Ensure good **financial management,** governance and value for money in all FM dealings across the portfolio. This includes weighing up the relative value of owned vs. leased buildings.
- Manage and negotiate all FM **contracts,** in conjunction with the SCM Department.
- Set the standard for **Corporate Social Responsibility** and **sustainable use of resources,** including energy and water

usage and other environmental policies (see also CSR chapter).

- Oversee the **implementation of Facilities-related projects** – this will range from acquisition and disposal, to building refurbishments, to ongoing preventive maintenance.

> Good Facilities managers will be highly commercial in nature, assessing the benefits of ownership vs. leasing and advising you on the optimum long-term Facilities strategy for the organisation.

- Maintain the **buildings asset registers** and the operating and maintenance manuals for all properties owned.
- Design the **building internal environment** as a mirror for the organisation's culture – collaborative, conservative, flexible, innovative or creative.
- Optimise the use of **internal space** through good planning.
- May oversee **other employee offerings,** such as gym or retail space.
- Manage **building security** – physical security and the resilience of power and utilities.
- May manage **catering** arrangements.
- Contribute to the organisational **change agenda**, ensuring Facilities changes are communicated, consulted on and managed in collaboration with staff to promote optimal acceptance and usage.
- Oversee the Facilities-related **risk agenda**, highlighting risks and developing mitigation plans.

> Facilities acts as a strong advocate to senior management on what needs to be done to preserve and protect the organisation's real estate and, more importantly, the safety and well-being of its people.

- Ensure facilities are **inclusive and accessible** to all staff.
- Provide **service management** and respond to employee requests and concerns.
- Build **quality** into all FM processes.
- **Monitor and report** back on facilities issues, health & safety issues, incidents and business continuity / disaster recovery planning and testing.
- **Ensure compliance** with all relevant building regulations, regulatory and statutory requirements.

Facilities and the link to organisational strategy

FM is at its most effective when it aligns with, complements and contributes to the overall strategy of the organisation. Many Facilities managers feel they're a long way from the CEO – an unloved cost centre charged with the less glamorous roles. Breaking that cycle and giving the FM department an insight into the future of the organisation will yield higher-order planning and deeper insights. The RICS[50] represents this relationship to strategy as follows:

---

[50] "Strategic Facilities Management." RICS Professional Guidance, Global. October 2013. Accessed June 10, 2017. http://www.rics.org/Global/Strategic_Facilities_Management_2nd_edition_PG guidance_2013.pdf.

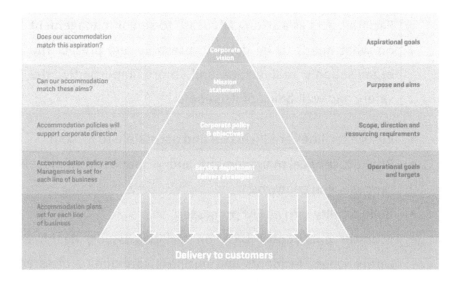

The FM team needs to know about the growth and divestment plans of the organisation. What business lines are strategic and may get larger? What is tailing off or needs a lower cost proposition? What activities need to be in high cost centres? What can be moved out? What's happening to the headcount? What proportion of the staff is fixed and what will fluctuate? Is the organisation in growth mode, looking for prestigious new sites? Or is it looking to pull back, to realise some cash from non-performing business lines and make efficiencies? This is sensitive information, not to be shared widely, but your Head of FM should be in that circle of people who "need to know".

As COO you set the tone for how seriously rest of the organisation takes FM. From their reporting line, to the decisions they're privy to, to how early they're involved in decision-making – your role is to give FM the respect and the access it needs to go from delivering a baseline operational capability to becoming a bona fide strategic partner. Through your breadth of access, you can also ensure that Facilities has access to other parts of the organisation as I outline below.

Overlaps

Expect FM to work with Finance on buildings-related cost analysis and procurement decisions. They should have a close working relationship with Risk and IT on business resilience, including decisions on failover sites, IT backup and restore procedures, and testing. They'll need a tight relationship with IT on issues such as connectivity / network strength, server storage, and decisions around desktop provision and power supplies. Finally, there should be an ongoing dialogue with the SCM department on acquisition, lease and disposal costs of buildings. And if any building services are outsourced, they'll need the support of SCM to meet quality and cost requirements.

Relationships to watch

FM can sometimes be the weaker partner to the better-known IT department and can struggle to push back on IT's ever-growing requirements. This can result in IT progressing with their acquisitions and FM finding out too late that that new server requires a dedicated air conditioning unit in a new raised-floor sealed room. Foster communication between these two teams, and task them with understanding the full costs of new IT investments.

It's important FM talks to HR. When staff have health issues or require special arrangements, or when they're discontented over a festering issue, timely interaction between these two departments can head off a lot of issues before they escalate.

Facilities and the link to people

If you ask a Facilities consultancy to assess your organisation, they'll start with demographics.

I was surprised to see a staff survey on facilities contain questions about the age of staff and whether they considered themselves introverts or extroverts. This additional analysis provided a fascinating insight into personality types and how they viewed and used their office space. It showed which departments were more satisfied with their working environments, and which were less. It sorted responses by generation – Baby Boomers, Generation X and Millennials – then by personality types.

When overlaid with the organisational culture (open, closed, collaborative, thoughtful, learning), this type of analysis will provide you with an in-depth picture about how your organisation wants to work, and whether the facilities on offer are servicing that, or getting in the way and causing daily irritations.

People want to work in different ways at different times. Sometimes we all need silence and exclusion for deep thought. Sometimes we want to bounce ideas off each other and build energy. What this points to is the need for different types of space throughout the office. We know that sitting at our desks for eight hours a day is terrible for our general health and wellbeing and that we should get up and walk around at least every 45 minutes. Our office space should complement these needs.

Industry frameworks

At time of writing, a new ISO 41000 is an eagerly anticipated work in progress. Without it, FM is a body of a number of different disciplines. The RICS has published a guidance note on strategic FM. It lists several other ISO and related standards, including:

- EN ISO 9000 Quality management systems — Fundamentals and vocabulary (ISO 9000:2005)
- ISO 14001 Environmental management systems
- ISO 15392 Sustainability in building construction — General principles
- ISO 15686-5 Buildings and constructed assets — Service-life planning — Part 5: Life cycle costing
- ISO 28000:2007 specifies the requirements for a security management system, including those aspects critical to security assurance of the supply chain
- NS 3454 Life cycle costs for building and civil engineering work — Principles and classification
- BS8536 2010 Facility management briefing, Code of practice
- BS8572 2011 Guide to the procurement of facility-related services

The British Institute of Facilities Management is a useful resource and contains a professional standards framework and handbook as well as the following set of standards, which have pan-European application:

- BS EN 15221-1 Facilities Management: terms and definitions

- BS EN 15221-2 Guidance on How to Prepare Facility Management Agreements
- BS EN 15221-3 Guidance on Quality in Facilities Management
- BS EN 15221-4 Taxonomy, Classification and Structures in Facilities Management
- BS EN 15221-5 Guidance on Facilities Management Processes
- BS EN 15221-6 Area and Space Measurement in Facilities Management
- BS EN 15221-7 Guidelines for Performance Benchmarking in Facilities Management

The main legislation in the UK is the Health and Safety at Work Act 1974, supplemented by the Construction Design and Management Regulations of 2007. For a fuller list of UK legislation and regulations relating to Health & Safety, see the RICS guidance.

The Employers' Liability (Compulsory Insurance) Act 1969 requires employers to take out insurance against accidents and ill health affecting their employees.

Warning signs

You should be on the lookout for the following:

No facilities strategy, or the FM team unaware of the corporate strategy. This indicates a lack of joined-up thinking and / or FM being not highly regarded by the organisation.

Dilapidated, ill-maintained buildings. If what you can see is bad, then what about the things you can't see?

A significant number of **safety issues / concerns / complaints**.

A large number of retail premises with long tie-ins and questionable profitability. This indicates a possible lack of commercial awareness of the costs of premises, insufficient governance, or facilities being browbeaten by the sales agenda.

Lack of governance around entering into new buildings contracts.

Overly **high facilities costs** or **benchmarking of costs not performed**. This indicates a possible lack of commercialism on the part of FM.

Good to great

A strong FM team is strategic and commercial in nature. The staff are aware of market trends and new opportunities. They'll come to you with suggestions on how to create value, get more out of existing space or forego costs. They'll bring you solutions that take into account the cost of decisions over the entire lifecycle of assets, and consider the interplay of different factors to give you a multi-dimensional view of the impact of these enormous facilities decisions.

Good Facilities managers are plugged into the culture of the organisation, into what people talk about (in Barclays the ultimate perk was having your own waste basket; in Save the Children the ongoing complaint was about the constant lack of spoons). Seemingly small things can become little cultural beacons and enter the employee lexicon. In response to employee feedback, good Facilities managers will flex their limited budgets and try to address the pain points.

Although demonstrating value for money is an important aspect to benchmark on, enlightened Facilities managers will provide Management a more rounded view of performance than just costs and preventive maintenance. They'll show the benefits in terms of employee satisfaction and productivity, organisational brand, etc. The RICS suggests a balanced scorecard approach[51] which, as well as these aspects, seeks to recognise and reward continuous improvement, innovation and learning.

Current hot topics

Building Information Modelling ("BIM") is the cool trend in Facilities at the moment. It's the digitisation of the physical building space in 3D for better insight into space management, planning, usage and evacuation procedures. The challenge is the cost and effort in putting it in place, and the need to integrate it with existing systems.

Flexible space to rent. Organisations such as WeWork offer flexible workspace, provide networking opportunities, free beer (!) and other perks which go down incredibly well with employees. They can be expensive, but given their growth trajectory, they're clearly popular and serve a useful purpose.

---

[51]http://www.rics.org/Global/Strategic_Facilities_Management_2nd_edition_P
Gguidance_2013.pdf

Kick back from open plan / hot desking. There's a bit of a reaction to open plan and hot desking as the best way to work at the moment. It can lead to distraction and wasted time searching for space. It limits privacy and it's hard to find space for conference calls. While few believe this heralds a return to cubicles and offices for everyone, there is a recognition that it's all in the blend. Dave Coplin's book *"Business reimagined: Why work isn't working and what you can do about it"* is a brilliant read on this subject.

> Warning: remember, you'll never please everyone. So, get it as good as you can for the majority and know when to stop.

Teleconferencing vs. travel. From Skype for Business to high-end "telepresence" (where it feels as if the person is across the table from you, and you can reach out and grab their coffee), the experience of interacting with people around the world is improving all the time. More sophisticated facilities can require significant investment - the trick is to ensure there is a corresponding reduction in the travel bill and that the ROI is achieved.

Working remotely. Working remotely is also on the increase. FM teams need to work with HR and IT to model what proportion of employees will be in the building on any given day, and work with HR and Management to find the optimal desk allocation. Since you don't usually need to encourage people to work from home on a Friday, you'll find your buildings highly occupied early in the week and tailing off afterwards.

Checklist of policies

- Environmental policy
- Security / health & safety policy

Ten questions to ask

1. What is the inventory of properties held by the organisation and are they freehold or leasehold? Where are the properties located? What is their market value?

2. What are the major upcoming dates with regard to lease renewals and rent reviews?

3. Is there a vision for corporate real estate? Is it about prestige and/or maximising value? Does it match the culture and the strategy of the organisation?

4. Is everything in the building within regulations? Have all assets been maintained in accordance with prescribed standards? Is there a planned preventive maintenance schedule?

5. How many safety incidents have been reported in the past year?

6. Is management happy with the reception experience for visitors? Does it contribute to the organisation's brand and proposition?

7. What do staff think of the responsiveness and quality of the facilities management service?

8. How is FM performance reported to Management? What reports do they receive to drive their decisions?

9. What access does FM get to the Executive team, to the Board?

10. What strategic acquisitions / divestments / upgrades are currently planned? What's the governance around these decisions? Who makes the final call and how?

Further reading

Coplin, D. *"Business reimagined: Why work isn't working and what you can do about it"*, Harriman House, 2013

Weiss, D., "Why is Facilities Management Struggling to be Strategic?"

http://www.bifm.org.uk/bifm/professionaldevelopment/prostandards

"Strategic facilities management." *RICS Professional Guidance*

15. INTERNAL COMMUNICATIONS & PUBLIC RELATIONS

What this department does

This department (or departments, if they're separate) handles your internal and external communication. It projects your brand, engages your people and broadcasts your message. Effective communication is fundamental to your success and that of your organisation.

A change has happened in the workforce in recent years. Trust is in much shorter supply. Internal Communications has a key role to play in educating, informing, engaging and motivating your people. It can project you and the Management team in the best light – or not. The days of closed, obedient, command and control environments are behind us. The upcoming generation of workers has grown up in a digital, reality-TV-driven and highly personalised world where they want to feel in control. They seek out experiences over a job. They want to contribute to a purpose that makes them feel good and valued, and may move on quickly if it gets stale. They want to feel empowered, engaged and motivated in a culture of equality and innovation. They want their thoughts, opinions and ideas to be heard, or they'll simply walk. And they will talk to their friends about the organisation. When motivated and engaged, they are your most powerful and authentic ambassadors. When disenfranchised, they can weaken your employee proposition and your brand. Engaging them in transparent and honest two-way dialogue is critical to success.

Similarly, how organisations engage with their customers, the public, the media, regulators and other key stakeholders has had to change. Your Public Relations ("PR") team assesses the mood and concerns of these groups and crafts both proactive and reactive plans to communicate with them. In a world of viral, instantaneous communication, news – both good and bad – travels fast. PR failures are quickly and publicly punished. You can do everything else right, but get this wrong, and your efforts will be for naught.

Often COOs are uncomfortable with communications, particularly with external communications. If this is a part of your role, you can seek out some external media training, which is a great confidence booster.

It's a truism to say that an organisation is little more than the quality of its people. Yet, Internal Communications is frequently neglected, or populated with teeth-clenching corporate nonsense. Cut though the jargon, find your organisation's tone of voice, find *your* tone of voice and let that shine through. A great book on finding your authentic voice is *Gravitas: Communicate with Confidence, Influence and Authority* by Caroline Goyder.

Roles and responsibilities – Internal Communications

Strategy and planning

- **Explain the strategy and the role staff play in it.** At its core, employee motivation stems from each and every person understanding the "why" behind the strategy and their role in in delivering it. We've all heard the adage about the janitor at NASA who identified his mission as sending people to the moon. The Internal Communications strategy should outline how the overarching goals of the organisation are being translated into tangible, practical and implementable actions for everyone.

- **Create a communications strategy that links to the organisational strategy.** This should be clear on the Communications roles of the CEO, the COO, the Executive team, Non-Executive Directors and others. The Communications strategy forms the backbone for a consistent set of messages. I've seen the damaging, corrosive effect of siloed communications, where departmental managers thought they had a better set of messages than the organisational one. When this happens, staff from different departments talk to each other, compare what's being said and infer that it's all lies or that Management doesn't know what they're doing. A skilled Head of Internal Communications will take the time to build relationships with all departments and harness the best of the messaging, frameworks and tools from across the organisation — then use a single set for the common good. As COO you need to impress upon your Executive team the importance of consistency of message.

- **Internal Communications objectives.** It is important that the Internal Communication team knows what it's trying to achieve. It is to inform? To motivate and inspire? To deliver tough news? To help foster a change in culture or sense of belonging? To manage through a crisis?

- Creating a **Communications calendar** for the year ahead, showing the main set pieces and ensuring key events don't overlap.

Understand and amplify the culture

- **Conveying and explaining the organisation's vision, mission and values.** Internal Communications taps into the culture of the organisation, amplifying and reinforcing its history and values, and rewarding employees who espouse these values with recognition. This is a major driver of employee engagement.
- **Messaging, storytelling and design.** Internal Communications is responsible for crafting the messages that you and others will send out.
- **Divisional, tactical, departmental messages.** Internal Communications can segment the organisation into its constituent pieces by seniority, by division and by geography, and understand what drives them. Working with each to create the right blend of messaging, from the right people, across the most appropriate channels.
- **Consistent messages.** In his book *Winners: And How They Succeed*, Alastair Campbell said that a strategy should be capable of being expressed as a word, a phrase, a paragraph, a page, a speech and a book. The role of Communications is to build this messaging framework and content and to help Management reinforce it – consistently and often.
- **Facilitation of strategic events.** Linked to the overall communications plan, your Communications team will be

responsible for the running of key events – from town halls to staff social events. Part of this is ensuring an appropriate blend of management-led set pieces and employee-generated content (e.g., TED talks, lunch and learns) in order to meet your organisational objectives through a range of tactics, channels and media.

- **Specific support for projects and/or corporate events (merger, acquisition, redundancy, crises).** Whether it's the launch of a new system, a major moment in the organisation's life cycle or a crisis, Internal Communications should be on hand to consider what will be on employees' minds and to craft the right strategy to engage and inform them.

> **A note on accessibility.** Considering your audience and their accessibility needs as part of communications planning is a legal requirement. In the UK, the Equality Act 2010 protects disabled and other disadvantaged groups from discrimination in employment. If your communications are found to be discriminatory, your organisation could be liable. It's also the right thing to do, to promote a diverse and engaged workforce.

Tools, technology and digital

- **Maintenance of corporate resources,** such as the intranet, internal social media, blogs and other collateral. Invest in these areas and maximise using those that work best to talk to staff. When they work well, these platforms and tools save time and money, and give you all-important insight into what staff are interested in.

Feedback, coaching and facilitating

- **Feedback, reporting and monitoring.** The Internal Communications team should be an effective set of "eyes and ears on the ground", taking feedback from staff, understanding what messages are landing effectively, what staff want to hear more of and what unanswered questions they have.
- A trusted Internal Communications team will be able to understand the strengths and weaknesses of individual managers, what settings they do well in and where they struggle. Through a blend of coaching and channel selection, they can support Management to communicate through media that build on their strengths and present them in the most favourable light.

Overlaps

Internal Communications needs to have strong relationships with:

- HR – who are also an important channel in hearing the voices of employees.
- The Risk functions in reinforcing the key messages and helping with Compliance and awareness programmes.
- PR – to ensure consistency between internal and external messaging
- Marketing – Internal Communications has to reflect the external brand on the inside of the organisation.

Relationships to watch

One key relationship is between Internal Communications and the person responsible for the profile and messaging of the CEO. These two areas must be tightly connected, so there is consistency between the message the CEO is projecting, and the rest of the messaging in the organisation.

Roles and responsibilities – Public Relations

PR is about managing communications between an organisation and its external stakeholders, building and reinforcing a positive image of the organisation and dealing with events that could jeopardise that image. Its responsibilities include:

Strategy and planning

- Communicating the organisation's strategy, mission and vision externally
- Creating a PR strategy for key issues
- Detailed planning of key PR activities by day and by channel. You may hear your PR team refer to this as "the grid."
- Advising the CEO and Executive team on the PR implications of certain courses of action

Media relations

- Proactive outreach and securing "earned media" (which is publicity gained via promotional efforts vs. paid media advertising)

- Reactive media in response to the current news agenda or media enquiries
- Reputation and critical issues management

Creating messages that will resonate with the public and maintain the trust and credibility of your organisation. Crafting narratives and calls to action that will hit the public emotionally, on a personal level, causing them to connect with your brand and take the action you desire them to take (buy your product, donate to your cause etc.).

Management of digital and social media channels. Proactive and reactive management of social media channels, engaging with your stakeholders in their virtual meeting place of choice.

Executive profiling. Profiling senior executives in key publications, supporting them speaking at selected events, writing speeches, managing their social media. Tight definition of rights and responsibilities is important, as well as finding the right tone of voice. When I know a person, I can often tell whether it was they or someone from their team who has sent a tweet from their account, from a detail as small as an exclamation mark. It's important to be clear on social media whether the person is broadcasting on behalf of the organisation or in a "views-are-my-own" capacity.

Advisory. The brand and reputation of an organisation, and the public's trust in it are key determinants of its success. Your PR professionals should be considering the reputational risks that could arise as a result of actions taken by the organisation.

Reputation and organisation values should be actively used by them when advising Management.

Coaching senior stakeholders on media. Coordinating who will speak for the organisation. Ensuring they're "on message". Training and briefing key spokespeople to talk to the media, so that you have a bench of available people when needed.

Horizon scanning, monitoring the news agenda, public views and attitudes. What questions are customers and members of the public asking? Is the organisation answering them? Are others filling the vacuum? What trends and issues are likely to impact the organisation over the next decade that you need to start planning for now?

Reporting and feeding back. What messages are landing well with people? What is the public perception of the organisation? What are competitors doing that's resonating with your stakeholders? Using analytics, customer surveys, mystery shopping and polling are simple ways to seek feedback.

Overlaps

PR has natural overlaps with:

- Sales & Marketing – in promoting the organisation.
- The Digital team – in managing your website and other channels.
- Brand Marketing – in defining your organisation's brand personality, tone of voice and image.

Relationships to watch

The PR team must have access to Senior Management to discuss strategy – to understand where it's rooted and to advise on what elements may cause problems. The PR team can and should be an influential voice, advising the CEO on how certain messages could play out in the media.

Stakeholders

In order to craft the appropriate messages and achieve their goals, Internal Communications and PR teams must be clear about *who* they are communicating with, and what their concerns and issues are. The stakeholder list is often much more extensive than initially thought.

Internal stakeholders include

- Executive leadership
- The Board (which plays a leadership role in safeguarding the reputation of an organisation)
- Senior Management
- Culture carriers
- Project leads

External stakeholders include

- Shareholders
- The public
- The media
- Regulators
- Customers / beneficiaries
- Key influencers
- Politicians
- Policy makers

What's your personality going to be?

One thing you may need to consider for the first time as COO is how you want to come across, both internally and externally. What mobile channels will you be on? Will you be generating content? Will someone be doing it for you? Are your identities distinct from your role (e.g. @barackobama vs. @POTUS)? What content and messaging will you be known for? What followership do you have? Would it help the organisation for you to build one? Have you worked out a plan for your PR, starting with notification of your appointment?

Drivers of employee engagement:

To engage employees, you need to motivate them and to help them identify with the organisation's brand and values. Bolster their engagement with the messaging from your Internal Communications team. General drivers of engagement, which can be reinforced by Internal Communications are:

- Values
- Belief in strategic direction of organisation
- Belief in leadership
- Respect / equality / diversity
- Being heard
- Good people management
- Reward (less of a driver than we often think)
- Broader value proposition (work life balance, flexibility, etc.)

Channels

Channels are the conduits through which managers and staff communicate. It's important to give consideration to the most effective channel for each message. It's all too easy to fall into the trap of over-reliance on email – it's easy, it's instant, and it reaches everyone. However, a constant stream of emails will make your employees feel as if they're being talked "at" instead of talked "to." Work with your Internal Communications team to look at the broadest range of channel options to match the channel to the situation. Channels include:

- Written – emails, memos, desk drops, posters
- Face-to-face – large groups (town halls)
- Face-to-face – small groups (meetings at small round tables where staff get direct access to Management tend to generate high levels of engagement and positive feedback)
- Periodic communications – e.g., weekly bulletins
- Social media / blogging / online Q&As
- Ad hoc – staff-led events

Industry frameworks

Various frameworks, training courses and formal qualifications have been established to create and maintain standards in Internal Communications and PR.

- The Institute of Internal Communications has created a profession map[52] that lists six professional capabilities required by Internal Communications. They are:
  1. Organisational strategy and planning
  2. People and cultural understanding
  3. Messaging, storytelling and design
  4. Tools, technology and digital
  5. Coaching and facilitating
  6. Listening and measuring effectiveness
- In the UK, the <u>Chartered Institute of Public Relations</u> ("CIPR") offers training and qualifications in Internal Communications. They aim to create a predominantly chartered profession in PR, by achieving a critical mass of practitioners with the CIPR accreditation. The CIPR has a code of conduct based around three core principles: integrity, competence and confidentiality.
- Other professional Internal Communications associations include the <u>Institute of Internal Communication</u>, the <u>International Association of Business Communicators</u> (IABC) and others.

Monthly dashboard – suggested content

Your Internal Communications and PR team should provide your Management with regular metrics, including the following:

- Feedback from staff surveys

---

[52] Miller, Rachel. "Earn while you learn thanks to IoIC." All Things IC. March 15, 2017. Accessed June 12, 2017. http://www.allthingsic.com/ioiccpd/.

- Feedback from internal events
- What communications have been most accessed by employees online
- Key issues from any internal discussion boards
- Number of media mentions – positive, negative and neutral
- Number of hits by media outlet (e.g., radio, print, TV, online) and by geography
- Specific topics / pieces of coverage that have attained high readership / engagement
- Specific media interviews / documentaries
- Net promoter score or other customer satisfaction metrics

It's possible to infer the implied value of "earned media" from high quality content. However, be careful about overly focusing on this metric. The CIPR believes that the value of public relations is in strategic relationships, not in coverage. It is tempting for Management and the Board to assess PR in terms of the "value" of coverage, typically using Advertising Value Equivalent as a metric. The CIPR believes that AVE is flawed. They encourage COOs to evaluate PR outcomes more against business objectives - coverage is just one tool to build relationships and sustain reputations.

Warning signs

Internal Communications

No or little internal communication. If there is an information vacuum, employees will fill it with their own content.

Slow communication. When employees hear news on the grapevine long before it hits the official wires.

Fragmented communication. People getting different messages from different areas.

Overly top-down communication – and over-reliance on email.

Communication that doesn't ring true. Employees will smell it a mile off and be turned off by it. If not addressed, it can lead to cultural problems, cynicism and apathy.

A lack of purpose behind Internal Communications and what it's trying to achieve. Before issuing any communication or holding any event, think about your stakeholders and what you'd like them to "Think, Feel and Do" as a result of it.

PR

Bad PR – caused by PR or by the actions of the organisation. Sometimes it's not the issue itself that causes problems but the way it was handled that can cause the biggest PR problems.

Acrimonious media relationship. No matter how good the organisation's intentions, if this relationship isn't working, it'll be difficult to change the mind of the public.

PR team struggling to influence Management. There is nothing more dispiriting for the Head of PR than to tell a story they know will go down like the proverbial lead balloon. Counsel your CEO to listen to your PR team.

Good to great

With employees who are more mobile, informed, vocal and influential than ever before, your Internal Communications team has to go beyond traditional engagement. They need to harness your talent rather than speak at it. And they need to create powerful dialogue that furthers the goals of the organisation but that isn't driven from the top. In practice this means applying innovative solutions, re-examining the old ways of measuring success and leveraging the best technology available.

Great PR goes beyond creating a buzz about individual products or building a following. Great PR is about getting your organisation to be viewed as a thought leader, with an ethos (as well as products and services) that people genuinely love. It's about tapping into what your customers care about and providing opportunities for them to look clever by sharing your content. And it's about building a truly engaged network and growing the influence of your organisation.

Current hot topics

Moving beyond the traditional press release. In a crowded market place, organisations have to find new ways to engage and excite the public. As an innovative example, look at Blendtec videos on YouTube. To show the power of their blenders, Blendtec launched a series of "Will it Blend?" videos. In every video their blenders make powder out of everything from glow sticks to iPhones. Viral, inexpensive and very clever.

Integrated content. Written, video, infographics – reflecting all the different ways we consume information.

Minimum Viable Product – trying out different approaches and using analytics to see what is resonating. Particularly with social media, your PR team can try several approaches rather than banking on one, learn quickly and move forward.

Millennials. Millennials consume information differently and use devices differently (for example, 55% of millennials use voice commands daily). Your organisation needs to meet them in their chosen virtual locations, not put out content and hope they'll find it.

Slack, Facebook and other enterprise social networks (IBM connections, Yammer, Chatter, Jive, etc.). I recommend you choose one, and go with what employees instinctively like. If adopted, these networks can become a vibrant location for organisational connection.

Instant delivery, bypassing print. When a video can be instantly uploaded and a tweet instantly shared, organisations need to replicate these methods of sharing their content, or be left behind.

VR (Virtual Reality) as a marketing tool. Save the Children and other charities are pioneering the use of VR to bring a person on the street straight into a refugee camp or an education centre. Users are transported right into the situation where they can see their donations at work. This is a far more immersive experience than shaking a plastic bucket in people's faces.

Localism – the power of local reviews, anecdotal content and stories relevant to local communities. Global social networks can empower existing smaller communities and create new ones.

Big data and near-field communication technologies. Advertising boards will shortly have the ability to update as you're passing them, with content tailored just for you. An iBeacon can tell if someone who had downloaded your app has just entered a store and offer them instantaneous discounts or other incentives to buy.

Analytics for attribution and insight. What makes your customers click on a link in your email? What pages on your website turn them off and cause them to leave? Analytics tools on platforms such as Adobe will help you understand why your customers abandon their shopping carts and go elsewhere.

Ten questions to ask

Internal Communications

1. Who is responsible for Internal Communications?
2. What is the role and vision of Internal Communications?
3. Is there an Internal Communications plan and calendar?
4. How do Internal Communications feel they're viewed by the organisation? Are they involved at the outset of new ideas / ventures / issues, or are they told at the last minute?
5. Who are the good and natural communicators among the management team? Who stays out of the limelight?

6. What questions are employees asking (and what do people ask you when you meet them)?
7. What did the last staff survey say about Internal Communications, and what's being done about the feedback?
8. What are the current employee engagement levels, and what are their drivers?
9. What opportunities are there for staff to get involved and lead important conversations?
10. What access do staff have to Executive Management and the Board?

Public Relations

1. What are the stated aims of the media team? How is success measured?
2. What is the media strategy? To be proactive? To stay out of the limelight?
3. What is the balance of positive and negative media stories about the organisation? How do you gauge stakeholders' views of the organisation?
4. What is the relationship with the media? Is the organisation viewed as an expert witness in its field and called upon to speak about matters? Or is it a difficult relationship?
5. Is there a "grid" of future proactive media events? Is there a positive PR plan?
6. To what extent, and in what settings are senior managers profiled?

7. What channels and settings is the organisation using to meet its stakeholders?
8. What audience analysis and targeting has been done? What channels are your customers using? Where are you "meeting" them?
9. What are the crisis management plans and protocols? Who is empowered to speak on behalf of the organisation, and who's their backup?
10. What is the decision-making process around how an organisation arrives at a "position" on a particular topic?

Checklist of policies

Media sign off policy: Who is empowered to speak on behalf of the organisation? What signoffs are required?

Crisis management procedures

Responsible / ethical communication policy

Copyright policy

Marketing to children / vulnerable people (see chapter 17)

Social media policy

Further reading

Goyder, C., Gravitas: Communicate with Confidence, Influence and Authority

https://www.cipr.co.uk/content/policy-resources/toolkits-and-best-practice-guides

https://www.cipr.co.uk/sites/default/files/CIPR%20Social%20Media%20Guidelines%202013.pdf

www.gov.uk/dwp/disabilityconfident

http://engageforsuccess.org/wp-content/uploads/2015/10/Melcrum-Inside-Internal-Comms-1.pdf

http://www.mckinsey.com/industries/high-tech/our-insights/the-social-economy

https://blog.enplug.com/17-internal-communications-best-practices-for-2017

16. SUSTAINABILITY

What this department does

You're reading this book because you want to be an effective COO – a respected leader who inspires your people and organisation. You want to drive sustainable success for the future, address stakeholder interests and balance short-term results with long-term success. You want to be a good COO – ethical, progressive and thoughtful – and to leave a legacy of a better organisation and a better world. This is where your CSR (Corporate Social Responsibility) / Sustainability Department comes in. Both terms are frequently used – I will use "Sustainability" in this book.

Sustainability goes way beyond having a recycling policy. It looks at the impact your organisation is making on the world as a whole. This includes your products and services, your partnerships with other organisations, your R&D, volunteering and other participation opportunities. Increasingly, it looks at your organisation's overall value proposition and whether it is delivering social value in the world. If you want to appeal to your customers and to attract the next generation of talent, you must address Sustainability.

Sustainability is no longer just a "nice to have". Progressive Boards, and indeed the capital markets - mainstream stock markets, private equity, pension funds and others - increasingly view it as a sign of good corporate governance and therefore essential.

The objective of Sustainability is to embed social, governance and environmental considerations into core decision-making and operational processes. As COO you'll play a central role as an advocate and a catalyst for putting sustainability where it belongs – in the core of your organisation.

Roles and responsibilities

- Setting the Sustainability strategy
- Aligning management and staff behind principles and engaging them
- Setting social, environmental and governance policy; helping to embed this in the day-to-day decision-making processes
- Setting the agenda for Diversity & Inclusion (might also sit in HR)
- Defining the strategy for engaging with partners. The relationships between public, private and third sectors have changed. It's now about collaborative problem solving – bringing together a combination of unique, complimentary skills and capabilities to solve big challenges and engender mutually successful outcomes.
- Reviewing all aspects of the organisation for alignment with principles and proposing improvements
- Reporting on Sustainability. Focusing on authentic communications. Avoiding "greenwash" which is falsely presenting an environmentally-friendly image.

> **The CIPR identifies seven causes of "greenwash"[53]:**
>
> 1. The pressure to differentiate products in order to sell more
> 2. Culture / pride – desire to show an organisation in its best light and hide or minimise issues
> 3. Mistaking aspirations for real action
> 4. Being "enthusiastic but uninformed"
> 5. Enthusiasm to communicate, before all the necessary proof points are in place
> 6. Being vague or ambiguous
> 7. The temptation to use "green" as a reputation enhancer

Overlaps and Relationships to watch

An effective Sustainability team should work with:

- HR in setting the diversity and human / labour rights agenda
- Facilities on environmental issues – from energy saving to recycling
- Operations / Manufacturing on sustainable practices
- SCM on ethical and local sourcing
- R&D and Sales & Marketing on fostering relationships and partners

---

[53] "CIPR Best Practice Guidelines for Environmental Sustainability Communications." *CIPR*

Industry frameworks

ISO 14000 is a set of standards covering environmental performance.

In the UK, the Environmental Protection Act 1990 defines the duty of care of all "waste producers", which means pretty much all organisations. It's the responsibility of all organisations to manage their waste safely and responsibly. Non-compliance is a criminal offence and carries punitive fines. In England and Wales, regulation is enforced by the Environmental Agency. In the US, the Environmental Protection Agency is charged with "protecting human health and the environment by writing and enforcing regulations based on laws passed by Congress". The EU has a huge range (over 500 Directives, Regulations and Decisions) of environmental law.

Reporting Frameworks – the Global Reporting Initiative

The Global Reporting Initiative ("GRI") sets sustainability reporting standards[54] that are respected and observed around the world. They cover economic, environmental and social topics, and are modular, so you can tackle them one at a time or holistically.

GRI 101 explains how to use and reference the standards, and how to report in accordance with them. It defines principles for defining report content and quality.

---

[54] *GRI* standards: https://www.globalreporting.org/standards

Principles for report content	Principles for report quality
✓ Stakeholder inclusiveness	✓ Accuracy
✓ Sustainability context	✓ Balance
✓ Materiality	✓ Clarity
✓ Completeness	✓ Comparability
	✓ Reliability
	✓ Timeliness

The reporting framework gives you two options – to comply with the core standards or with the comprehensive framework. Where you don't comply, you should explain why.

"GRI 102 – General disclosures" specifies the disclosures that must be made in order to be GRI compliant. These include organisational profile, strategy, ethics and integrity, governance, stakeholder engagement and reporting practices.

"GRI 103 – Management approach" outlines how to report how Management is dealing with Sustainability topics. It requires you to explain your policies, commitments, goals and targets, responsibilities, resources, grievance mechanisms and details of particular supporting projects and programmes.

Beyond that, GRI links to a series of technical standards across three areas – economic, environmental and social – on topics from water usage to corruption, from child labour to security. You choose the ones that are relevant to you and then report on your organisation's current status against the standard. Each standard contains clearly marked requirements, recommendations and guidance.

Warning signs

Lack of Sustainability strategy. Indicating this is not a priority for the Board or Management. The issue *is* likely to be a priority for customers and for regulators? Sustainability is increasingly viewed as a core competency and standing agenda item at Board level. If your organisation hasn't reached that realisation, you'll need to usher it along.

Dissonance between the views and interests of staff and Management on Sustainability. Management may find their people quite engaged on this – sometimes it just takes some senior sponsorship to kick-start the effort.

A **history of bad PR relating to Sustainability.** This means your organisation will have to work hard to change its reputation.

Good to great

You know Sustainability is humming when:

- It's positioned within the organisation's long-term strategy, business plans, risks, opportunities and mission as a source of innovation and new ideas.
- You're using your best minds and R&D people to further social good as part of your mission.
- You've broadened your definition of success beyond financials. Initially a voluntary option, financial markets are increasingly looking for a broader set of metrics to gauge performance.

- You and your CEO feel empowered to discuss social good, as opposed to being slaves to quarterly economic performance reporting. Unilever CEO Paul Polman has given shareholders clear expectations regarding Unilever's sustainability-first agenda[55]. He abolished quarterly earnings reports and stated that he wanted Unilever to become "the biggest NGO in the world."

Sustainability leaders look to the core of their organisation and re-engineer its very purpose to make the world better. True Sustainability is about innovation and new business models – not just risk mitigation. Organisations such as Nike, Unilever, Patagonia and GE are defining new markets and new ways of working.

Nike[56] wants to double its business and halve its environmental impact via three strategies:

- Minimise environmental footprint
- Transform manufacturing
- Unleash human potential

Patagonia[57] charts its journey from realising the damaging effects of pesticides on cotton to managing the balance between growth and consumption.

Ecomagination[58] is **GE's** growth strategy to "enhance resource productivity" and reduce environmental impact on a global scale via its commercial solutions.

---

[55] http://fortune.com/2017/02/17/unilever-paul-polman-responsibility-growth/
[56] http://about.nike.com/pages/sustainable-innovation
[57] http://www.patagonia.com/sustainability.html

When you position social good at the core of your organisation, Sustainability becomes transformational. Most organisations don't even come close to this, but the ones that do are truly inspiring.

In the HBR article "Lessons from Companies That Put Purpose Ahead of Short-Term Profits," Andrew White talks about how leaders *accept* the paradoxes of balancing economic success and social good, then *confront* and *transcend* them[59]. I summarise these below, together with my reflections.

Accept:

- Identify *all* your stakeholders and their expectations. This can be surprising. For example, if you are a high street bank or a post office, there are deeply engrained expectations of your role that have nothing to do with what your shareholders want.
- Acknowledge conflicting expectations – this is uncomfortable but necessary.

Confront:

- Reach out to negative stakeholders. Unlikely alliances have been forged when organisations have embraced their greatest naysayers.

---

[58] https://www.ge.com/about-us/ecomagination

[59] White, Andrew. "Lessons from Companies That Put Purpose Ahead of Short-Term Profits." *Harvard Business Review*, June 9, 2016. Accessed June 14, 2017. https://hbr.org/2016/06/lessons-from-companies-that-put-purpose-ahead-of-short-term-profits.

- Accept that this is a long game. It will take a long time to shake off the bad-guy mantle.

Transcend

- Create new labels. Re-categorise success. Define new terms.
- Make decisions. What are you doing to start and stop doing? Put actions over words.

The author is right when he says: "The outcome of this process is not a polished statement of purpose - but significant decisions grounded in a deep understanding of purpose characterized by a quiet sense of service to something greater than the immediate needs of customers and short-term demands of investors." If you can achieve that, there is no greater service you'll do for the organisation, or the world.

Current hot topics

Social innovation. Using innovation to create entirely new business models (or to pivot from current models), to create new markets as well as social and environmental value. Organisations doing this ensure their continued relevance and success in a fast-changing world.

Modern slavery. New legislation has placed increased demands on organisations to scrutinise their supply chains and ensure they're not inadvertently supporting this abhorrent practice.

Reporting on Sustainability. Auditors and accountants are considering new ways of reporting corporate performance, taking

Sustainability into account. From integrated reports combining financial and non-financial measures of success to full-blown sustainability accounting, this is an evolving area.

Ten questions to ask

1. Does the organisation have a Sustainability strategy?
2. How genuine is it? Is it a PR exercise to make the organisation look good? Or is it linked with core vision, mission and values?
3. Are staff engaged in the Sustainability strategy? What opportunities do they have to contribute, beyond an annual fundraising event? Are they able to give their time? Can they be seconded?
4. Who are the organisation's major stakeholders? What's important to them?
5. Who does the organisation partner with on Sustainability?
6. Does Management believe in the value of Sustainability?
7. Is Management incentivised to drive the Sustainability agenda and serve as accountable advocates?
8. What, at the essence of what your organisation does, could be tweaked, adapted, furthered in order to do good in the world?
9. How does the organisation measure success? Are there alternative models that sit alongside P&L and share price?
10. What reporting is done on Sustainability? Is it meaningful?

Further reading

ISO 14000 – Environmental performance https://www.iso.org/iso-14001-environmental-management.html

GRI standards: https://www.globalreporting.org/standards

"CIPR Best Practice Guidelines for Environmental Sustainability Communications." *CIPR*

White, A., "Lessons from Companies That Put Purpose Ahead of Short-Term Profits." *Harvard Business Review*, June 9, 2016

http://www.undp.org/content/undp/en/home/sustainable-development-goals.html

OECD Guidelines for Multinational Enterprises 2011 Edition by Organisation for Economic Cooperation and Development

The Extractive Industries Transparency Initiative "The global standard for the good governance of oil, gas and mineral resources." EITI. https://eiti.org/

Business for Social Responsibility https://www.bsr.org/en/our-insights

"Webinar: 2017 Sustainability Trends – Impacts for Corporate Leadership." SustainAbility. http://sustainability.com/our-work/insights/webinar-2017-sustainability-trends-impacts-corporate-leadership/

17. SAFEGUARDING OF VULNERABLE PEOPLE

Safeguarding is a sensitive topic and you may not think it applies to you, your organisation or sector. However, it is relevant in more cases than people think. If you're a hotel chain, children walk in and out of your doors every day. If you market products online, you may be marketing to children. If your ads feature pictures of happy families using your products, you're using images of children and need to follow the right protocols. Awareness is the strongest protection we can offer children and vulnerable individuals. I will mostly speak about child safeguarding as I know this area best, the same concepts apply to other vulnerable parts of the population.

Once you're sensitised to child safeguarding, know where it applies and understand how it can go wrong, you can never take it for granted again. As the mother of two small children, when I joined Save the Children UK, I felt an immediate responsibility for every child we were helping. I observed that, if we pull children from the rubble of an earthquake and administer life-saving medication, but afterwards they go back to being exploited or abused, then have we really saved them?

When I joined Save the Children, I wasn't initially responsible for Child Safeguarding. It was viewed as a specialist area that sat within HR. Within a short period of time though, and with their agreement, I took it on – it needed someone in a position to join the dots across different departments and ensure we were doing all we could, in the most consistent and coherent way.

Roles and responsibilities

If your organisation needs to safeguard parts of the population, your team should have the following responsibilities:

- Setting an overall direction and strategy for safeguarding
- Setting policy and associated procedures
- Conducting training and awareness
- Reviewing processes (e.g. on-boarding of staff, signing off marketing material)
- Creating action plans to mitigate areas of weakness
- Responding to concerns raised
- Putting procedures and systems in place for case management
- Monitoring and reporting
- Liaising with the relevant authorities

Overlaps / relationships

Safeguarding needs to have a close relationship with HR, especially when on-boarding new employees. HR will help you ensure the staff you hire have appropriate backgrounds.

The Risk team will help with setting frameworks and responding to concerns.

Sales & Marketing will help with the use of imagery, permission seeking, and marketing to children.

Industry frameworks

There is a large body of literature on safeguarding in different sectors, from nursing to education. The CIPR has published a best practice guide[60] on communicating with children. The UK Advertising Standards Authority (ASA) regulates commercials and has developed codes of practice. The UK Department of Health has guidelines on food and drink advertising and marketing to children. In the USA, the Children's Online Privacy Protection Act 1998 (COPPA) regulates online services and children's online privacy.

The Canadian Centre for Child Protection Inc., has a very accessible suite of products, including the Commit to Kids programme[61] which outlines a ten point plan for making an organisation safe for children.

1. Assess your organisation – where could it be exposed to risk?
2. Understand child abuse – including the potential for it to happen.
3. Manage risk through the development of an action plan.
4. Create a code of conduct for your people to sign up to.
5. Hire the right people – safe recruitment aims to prevent the wrong kind of people getting into the organisation in the first place.
6. Supervise and monitor – both formally and informally. Vigilant staff are the best protection.

---

[60] https://www.cipr.co.uk/content/policy-resources/toolkits-and-best-practice-guides/communicating-children

[61] http://www.commit2kids.ca/app/en/

7. Report abuse, misconduct, near misses and minor concerns. Foster a culture of openness, and ensure action is taken so people have faith in the process.
8. Write policies and procedures based on the specifics of the organisation.
9. Create a child protection manual – encompassing all elements to create multi-layered protection.
10. Train everyone (employees, volunteers, parents/guardians, children). The best systems are interdependent ones where everyone is reinforcing each other.

Checklist of policies

Your organisation should have the following Safeguarding policies at a minimum:

- On-boarding and vetting of new staff
- Code of conduct
- Policy for appropriate behaviour when in the company of vulnerable people
- Marketing to vulnerable people
- Use of imagery / permission
- Reporting concerns

Warning signs

You should be attuned to the following:

- A lack of awareness of the issue or a sense of "that doesn't happen around here."

- Lack of rigour around the procedures. This is an area that needs to be watertight.

- A fear of reporting concerns: "It's probably nothing. I don't want to get them into trouble – they're a good person". You need an open, no-blame culture where people feel empowered to raise even mild concerns.

- Words not deeds – Where people agree the topic is important, but it's not backed up by evidence, action or funding.

Case study: Olive Cooke

Olive Cooke was an elderly lady who had signed up over the years to various charities. Her details had been passed around on several mailing lists, resulting in her receiving dozens of letters from charities every week. Tragically, in May 2015 she took her own life. The resulting investigation highlighted the impact that regular bombardment by mail and telephone was having on her[62]. This was a wake-up call for the charity sector as a whole. Before this, the effects of contacting the public had been viewed as benign – no-one considered that it could cause a person distress. Charities responded by strengthening their charters around how donor data was collected and managed, and how a donor could opt-out of receiving communications. At the time of writing, the UK Fundraising Standards Board is looking at putting even more stringent provisions in place.

---

[62] http://www.bbc.co.uk/news/uk-england-bristol-35359268

Good to great

Proactive and "no blame" reporting and monitoring is a key component of a strong culture of safeguarding. Just as public transport passengers are encouraged to report their suspicions, your employees should be able to report something that seems relatively minor right now and have it dealt with sensitively, without fear of blame. Often, a minor drop in standards can be nipped in the bud before it becomes a significant concern.

Becoming a learning organisation. Organisations can be tempted to deal with an issue on a once-off basis and then brush it under the carpet. In doing so you'll miss the opportunity to ensure this particular issue never recurs. Your organisation must have a process for examining the root cause of something going wrong, for examining the underlying processes and systematically strengthening them (and training your people). Other issues may arise later, but there is no excuse for the same issue happening twice.

10 questions on Safeguarding

1. Do we have vulnerable sections of the population that we interact with / market to? When was a diagnostic last done?
2. Who is responsible for Safeguarding? What is their reporting line?
3. Is there a safeguarding code of conduct / policy?
4. Have we had any safeguarding incidents in the past?
5. Do staff receive safeguarding training?

6. What options are there for staff to report concerns (e.g. whistleblowing hotlines)?
7. What is the culture / attitude towards safeguarding?
8. Who is responsible for ensuring the suitability of products and services for customers?
9. Has the supply chain been thoroughly checked to ensure no child labour / bad labour practices?
10. Is safeguarding discussed at the Board and Executive Management meetings?

Further reading

https://www.protectchildren.ca/app/en/

https://www.cipr.co.uk/content/policy-resources/toolkits-and-best-practice-guides/communicating-children

"Protecting Children's Privacy Under COPPA: A survey on Compliance"

SECTION 3: PULLING IT ALL TOGETHER

In the beginning of the book I mentioned that as first-time COO you'll have gaps in your knowledge. I hope by now you have a much clearer sense of the 16 disciplines outlined in the previous chapters. Let's recount them: Culture, Strategy, Change, IT, Finance, Risk, Governance, Legal, HR, Compliance, Operations, Supply Chain Management, Communications & PR, Facilities and Safeguarding. Sounds like a lot, doesn't it? Do you feel comfortable talking about all of them? Most of them? Using the same criteria I outlined in Chapter 1, fill out the table below again to see how much you've learned.

Author's note: I'd love to know your before and after scores, and any thoughts you have on further content. Please email me your results at jennifer@coo-author.com. They'll influence what content I add to any future editions of the book.

Department	Before reading the book	After reading the book
Culture		
Strategy		
Change		
IT		
Finance		
Risk		
Governance		
Legal		
HR		

Compliance		
Operations		
Supply Chain Management		
Communications / PR		
Facilities / Real estate		
Safeguarding of vulnerable people		
Other		

You may be feeling overwhelmed right now. There is a lot of ground to cover, a lot to worry about and a lot to fix. In addition, leading these departments is only part of your role – you have a much broader role as one of the figureheads of the organisation. You have to forge relationships with your peers, your CEO, your Board. You need to introduce yourself to the organisation, set out your stall, and make your mark. How to do it all?

To be effective, you need to prioritise. In the next chapter, I'll give you some tools to do this. Also in this section, I'll talk about the role of the COO in unleashing innovation and agility in your organisation. Finally, I bring you back to your foundations – to considering your true purpose in this role. The formula for success in your role is already in your grasp. You just need to filter out the noise to find it.

18. Prioritisation and Focus

In your first 100 days as COO, nothing is more important than your ability to prioritise and to focus on outcomes. If you start your role with a massive, unprioritised to-do list and get drawn into endless "mandatory" meetings, you're not setting yourself up for success. Having prioritisation and focus in your life, and focusing on the outcomes the organisation needs will help ensure that, at the end of your first 100 days, six months, year and beyond, you can demonstrate real, tangible progress in the organisation.

- Prioritisation. Where will you direct your time, energy and political capital?
- Focus. What outcomes will you seek?

In *Your First 100 Days*, the author talks about ten roles you play as a senior executive: transition maker, unique contributor, content learner, business achiever, team builder, communications provider, value adder, relationship builder, culture navigator and market player. Your natural tendency may be to focus on the "business achiever" role, when in reality your role is much broader. She recommends that you specify a desired outcome for each of these ten roles, then break it down into 30-, 60- and 90-day targets. It's a highly effective system that has served me well.

In addition to this, look at each of the departments you're overseeing. Using the frameworks in this book, build a picture of the strengths and the weaknesses of every department, and the threats and opportunities that face it. Specify 3-5 objectives and agree them with the Heads of Departments. For the underperforming areas, get to the root cause of the issues and work out what remediation is required. For the areas that are thriving, think about how you can give them greater visibility, more responsibility, more opportunity.

Execute

Now that you know your goals, ensure they are reflected in what you actually spend your time doing. Work through your diary and strip out, as far as possible, anything that isn't serving your objectives. Colour code your diary if necessary to see how much of your time is being devoted to your goals and how much to things you feel you "have" to do. Have a five-minute conversation instead of a 30-minute meeting. Take your department head out for a mentoring coffee first thing in the morning instead of scheduling a meeting. Make the best use of your Executive Assistant / Chief of Staff. If necessary, get help from a professional coach.

Check, tweak, continue

How will you know whether your plans are working?

One of the first-time COO's key mistakes is not spending enough time on defining a system for checking progress. Any business analyst can put together a whizzy looking performance scorecard / dashboard with a RAG (Red, Amber, Green) status on it, but how often are they actually telling us anything of value?

Spend time with key staff, consider what real success looks like and put the right measures in place to demonstrate meaningful progress. Share your goals with your team – both personal and professional – and encourage them to do the same. Break objectives down into daily, weekly and monthly tasks. Be accountable to yourself in what you're looking to achieve.

19. Innovation and agility

Innovation and agility guard your organisation against extinction and irrelevance. They enable your organisation to evolve and grow.

> Innovation is the process by which organisations constantly evolve their offerings. Agility ensures there is enough flexibility in the organisation's strategy to respond to changes.

Innovation

As COO you need to foster an ecosystem within your organisation that is conducive to innovation. This means providing funding of course, but also developing a culture of openness, encouraging your people to try things, to create and let go of their creations if they're no good.

The degree of innovation and agility displayed by organisations varies greatly. Your approach will have to flex. A well-established, multi-national organisation faces markedly different challenges from those of a start-up. However, some principles can be applied to all situations. Seek to cultivate the following:

- A focus on a Minimum Viable Product
- Short cycle times (six weeks or less) to get new ideas off the ground
- Acceptance of failure
- An ability to pivot
- Avoiding over-prescribing the outcomes

- Respect for talent vs. individual ideas: when assessing new offerings, the much admired accelerator hub, Y Combinator, always favours great people and an OK idea over OK people and a great idea.

Innovation needs to become an ongoing, virtuous cycle, where your people try, fail, learn, pivot and start again. It means having a healthy "funnel" of ideas that constantly captures new content. This process needs to be easy and frictionless.

Innovation doesn't just apply to new products and services. For example, your approach to IT development can be agile and energetic, particularly on the user front end. Even if you're an established organisation with creaking systems in the background, you can master the twin-speed methodology and put leaner technologies in the hands of the front end users.

Agility

Heidrick & Struggles identify four capabilities[63] required for organisations to mobilise, execute and transform with agility. They are:

1. **Ripple intelligence.** The ability to keep abreast of the multiple, interdependent changes happening in the world and to understand the different ways they might interact and play out.

---

[63] Ruben Hillar, Colin Price, Sharon Toye, David Turnbull. "Accelerating performance: How to mobilise, execute, and transform with agility." *Heidrick & Struggles*

2. **Resource fluidity.** The skill of being able to constantly adjust the allocation of talent, resources and ideas to the most important challenges.
3. **Dissolving paradox.** Seeing past simplistic choices and recasting difficult decisions in ways that result in transformative, win-win outcomes.
4. **Liquid leadership.** Being able to operate (through hierarchy or other channels) to mobilise action and share information in the quickest way possible.

Your strategy needs to flex and adapt. McKeown[64] argues that "reacting is as important as planning." No strategy ever works out exactly as planned. No environment is without its changes – just look at the political environment in 2016. What determines ongoing success is how well your organisation reacts to changes.

When confronted with a game-changing situation, the questions to ask are:

- How fundamentally does this affect the strategy? Do we have to go back to the drawing board, completely, partially or not at all?
- What avenues has this opened up (as well as the ones it has potentially shut down)?
- How can we pivot from here?

---

[64] McKeown, M., *The Strategy Book, p27*

Further reading

McKeown, M., The Strategy Book

Hillar, R., Price, C., Toye, S., Turnbull, D.: "Accelerating performance: How to mobilise, execute, and transform with agility." *Heidrick & Struggles*

https://www.cipr.co.uk/content/policy-resources/toolkits-and-best-practice-guides/innovation-creativity

20. What's it all about anyway

I was always intrigued and terrified by Shel Silverstein's lyrics to the song "The Ballad of Lucy Jordan." It's a song about a 37-year-old woman who realised she'd never live her dream.

I think the world has improved for many of us since that song was written. People seem to feel more empowered now to seek out their own happiness. Attitudes towards age and what is possible have changed dramatically. At 42, I feel I have lots of options open for me.

However, when I was 37, several events in my life which shook me to my roots and changed me forever. I had borne two beautiful kids, and bringing them into the world and nurturing them made me realise that thousands and thousands of children don't have the same access to the fundamentals of life, health, education and protection. Then my Mum passed away from lung cancer at the age of 64. My Dad got seriously ill and almost died. Thankfully, due to his strength and positivity, he survived and is healthy and well again. Finally, I had a health scare which, while not serious in the short term, was the first time I was diagnosed as anything other than fighting fit.

All this gave me a dose of mortality like nothing I'd experienced before. All of a sudden, the realities of life and death were laid open to me, incontrovertible. There was nowhere to hide from the big questions. What was I put on this earth to do? Was I doing it? Was I making myself happy? Was I making others happy? Was I using the talents and the opportunities I was given? While my career thus far had made my husband and me comfortable, I didn't feel that I was making the world better. That led me to getting involved in our organisation's citizenship agenda, and eventually taking a role in a large global NGO, tasked with making the world better for children.

I tell you my story to prompt you to ask yourself these questions before embarking on your new role. Why are you doing it? Yes, to get paid and paid well, but why else? Are you driven by it? Is this the best use of your time, skills and energy? Are you motivated by the cause of the organisation and the impact it can have on the world? What difference can you make there? Doing soul searching and getting to the essence of why you are there will provide you with an iron core of "Why", which will give you energy and sustain you through the difficult days – because there are always difficult days.

I wish you joy, fulfilment and satisfaction in your new role. I hope this book fills in some of the gaps you may have been concerned about. Remember, nobody knows it all, and it's not your job to. Your job is to help your organisation understand what it's about and deliver it – as seamlessly and as sustainably as possible. If you can do this, your organisation will make the world better, make your employees' lives better and you will rest easy at night, knowing all is as it should be – perfectly imperfect.

ACKNOWLEDGEMENTS

Every effort has been made to trace the owners of copyright material. If there any omissions, please contact jennifer@coo-author.com

The author is grateful to the following publications for permission to reproduce copyright material.

The following articles are reprinted by permission of Harvard Business Review

"Second in Command: The Misunderstood role of the Chief Operating Officer", Bennett, N. & Miles, S.A., May 2006
"Why Strategy execution unravels, and what to do about it", Sull, Homkes & Sull, October 3, 2016
"Leading Change", Kotter, J., 1995
"The changing role of the CHRO", 2015
Copyright © by the Harvard Business Publishing Corporation; all rights reserved

UK Corporate Governance Code in chapter 10 © Financial Reporting Council Ltd (FRC). Adapted and reproduced with the kind permission of the Financial Reporting Council. All rights reserved. For further information, please visit www.frc.org.uk or call +44 (0)20 7492 2300.

GRI materials reproduced with the kind permission of GRI. GRI™ is an international independent organization that has pioneered corporate sustainability reporting since 1997. GRI helps businesses, governments and other organizations understand and communicate the impact of business on critical sustainability issues such as climate change, human rights, corruption and many others. With thousands of reporters in over 90 countries, GRI provides the world's most trusted and widely used standards on sustainability reporting, enabling organizations and their stakeholders to make better decisions based on information that matters. Currently, 38 countries and regions reference GRI in their policies. GRI is built upon a unique multi-stakeholder principle, which ensures the participation and expertise of diverse stakeholders in the development of its standards. GRI's mission is to empower decision-makers everywhere, through its standards and multi-stakeholder network, to take action towards a more sustainable economy and world.

The ten point plan in Chapter 17 is adapted from the *Commit to Kids - Program Overview Guide* that is available online at http://www.commit2kids.ca/pdfs/C2K_OverviewGuide_en.pdf accessed on June 20, 2017. Adapted with permission from the Canadian Centre for Child Protection Inc.

Thank you to the following wonderful authors for contributing such strong content, for allowing me to reference their material where permission was required, and for supporting a first-time author so graciously.

Adams, L.	"HR Disrupted: It's Time for Something Different"
Amor, M. & Pellew, A.	"The Idea in You: How to Find it, Build it and Change your Life"
Bridges, W.	"Managing Transitions: Making the Most of Change"
Campbell, A.	"Winners: And how they succeed"
Chapman & Sisodia	"Everybody matters: The Extraordinary Power of Caring for your People like Family"
Collins, J.	"Good to Great: Why some Companies Make the Leap and Others Don't"
Coplin, D	*"Business reimagined: Why work isn't working and what you can do about it"*, Harriman House, 2013
Drysdale, A.	"The Financial Controller"
Elrod, H.	"The Miracle Morning: The 6 Habits that will Transform your Life Before 8am"
Goyder, C	"Gravitas: Communicate with Confidence, Influence and Authority"
Kim, W & Mauborgne, R.	"Blue Ocean Strategy: How to Create Uncontested Market Space and Make the Competition Irrelevant"
McKeown, M.	"The Strategy Book"
Needle, D.	"Business in Context: An Introduction to Business and Its Environment"

O'Keeffe, N.	"Your first 100 days: How to make Maximum Impact in your New Leadership Role"
Parris, T.	"Chief of Staff: The Strategic Partner who will Revolutionize your Organisation"
Rowland, R. & Higgs, M.	"Sustaining Change: Leadership that Works"
Rumelt, R.	"Good Strategy, Bad Strategy: The Difference and Why it Matters"
Schein, E.H.	"Organizational Culture and Leadership", 5th ed.
Schulte, P.	"Complex IT Project Management: 16 steps to success"
Sinek, S.	"Leaders eat last: Why Some Teams Pull Together and Others Don't"
Sinek, S.	"Start with why: How Great Leaders Inspire Everyone To Take Action"
Turner, D.	"It's my pleasure: The Impact of Extraordinary Talent and a Compelling Culture"

COO diagram and seven core skills in Chapter 1 used with kind permission of Ernst & Young Global Limited © 2013 EYGM Limited.

Thank you to the following organisations for their highly relevant content:

Aberdeen Group

Axelos

British Institute of Facilities Management

Bill and Melinda Gates Foundation

Business for Social Responsibility

Chartered Institute of Public Relations

Deloitte

Department of Work and Pensions

Extractive Industries Transparency Initiative

EY

Faithful Gould

The Financial Times

Governance code steering group

Heidrick & Struggles

Hopkins University

In-house lawyer

ISACA

ISO

McKinsey

Melcrum (now part of CEB)

OECD

Royal Institution of Chartered Surveyors

SAI Global

Supply Chain Quarterly

SustainAbility

SELF-PUBLISHING
SCHOOL

NOW IT'S YOUR TURN

Discover the exact 3-step blueprint you need to become a bestselling author in 3 months.

Self-Publishing School helped me, and now I want them to help
you with this free webinar

Even if you're busy, bad at writing, or don't know where to start,
you CAN write a bestseller and build your best life.

With tools and experience across a variety niches and professions,
Self-Publishing School is the only resource you need to take your book to the finish line!

DON'T WAIT

Watch this FREE WEBINAR now, and
Say "YES" to becoming a bestseller:

https://xe172.isrefer.com/go/sps4fta-vts/bookbrosinc2241

14104046R00177